11+ Non-verbal Reasoning

WORKBOOK 6

Non-verbal Reasoning Technique

Dr Stephen C Curran
with Natalie Knowles
Edited by Katrina MacKay & Andrea Richardson

This book belongs to

ae PUBLICATIONS

Accelerated Education Publications Ltd

Contents

Chapter Twenty-three
RECOGNISING SHAPES

Shape Recognition involves the ability to identify the same shape: in a new position; after its fills have been changed; if it has been concealed amongst other shapes; once it has been disguised or modifed in some way.

Shape recognition includes the following question types:

Replica Figures • Silhouette • Reverse Fills • Jigsaw
Hidden Figure • Hidden Pattern • Fitting Shapes Inside
Assembling Figures • Adding Figures • Subtracting Figures
Folding a 2D Net • Unfolding a 2D Net

1. Replica Figures

Example: Which two figures are replica figures (exactly the same in every detail)?

a **b** **c** **d** **e**

Step 1 - Eliminate the figures with differences.

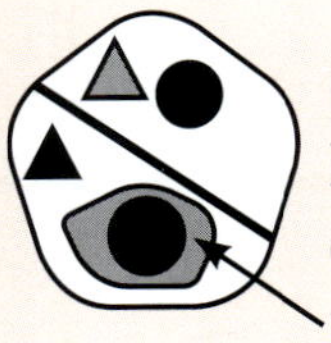

b has a larger Circle enclosed in this shape.

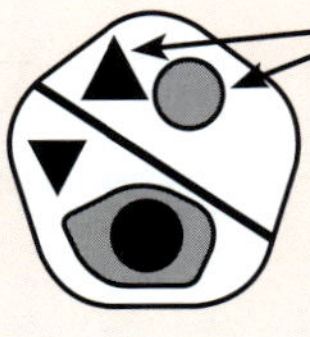

In **c** the Triangle has a Black Fill and the Circle has a Grey Fill.

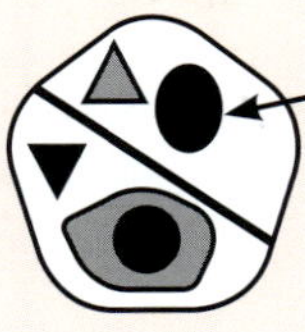

e has an Ellipse instead of a Circle.

Step 2 - Check the remaining two figures are identical.

If we compare **a** and **d** we can see they are identical to each other.

a  **d** 

Exercise 23: 1 Which two figures are replica figures?

1)

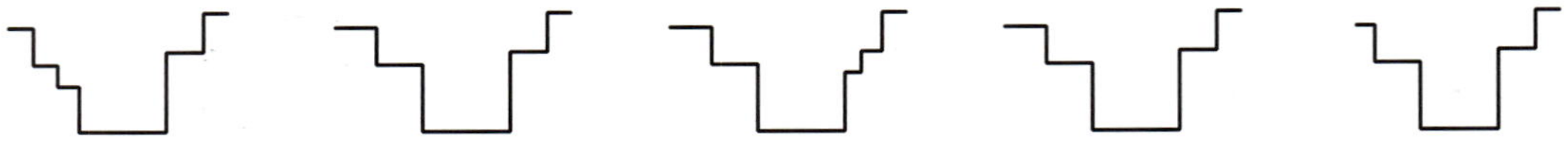

a b c d e

Answer ____ and ____

2)

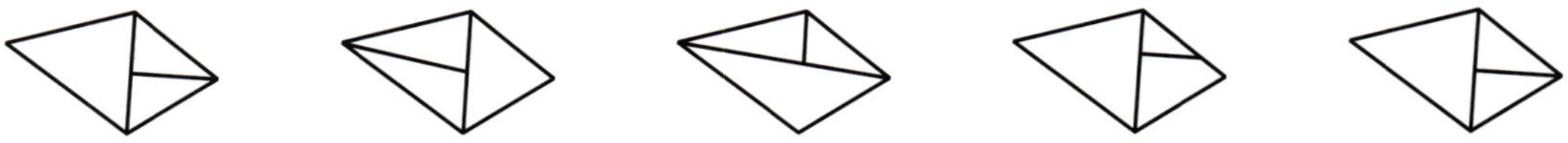

a b c d e

Answer a and e

3)

a b c d e

Answer b and c

4)

a b c d e

Answer B and E

5)

a b c d e

Answer a and c

6) 

a b c d e

Answer c and e

7) 

a b c d e

Answer a and d

8) 

a b c d e

Answer b and e

9) 

a b c d e

Answer a and e

10) 

a b c d e

Answer a and c

Score

2. Silhouette Type 1

Silhouette questions are very similar to Replica Figures questions, except all areas of the figure that are not White receive a Black Fill. White Fills of a silhouette are regarded as see-through.

Example: Which figure on the right is a silhouette of the Test Figure?

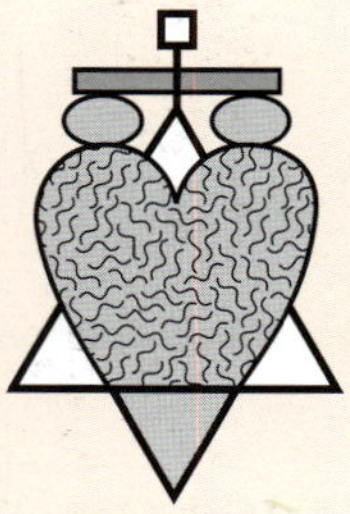

Test Figure

a

b

c

d

Step 1 - Look for any silhouettes that do not match the outline of the Test Figure as this is easier to spot than incorrect fills.

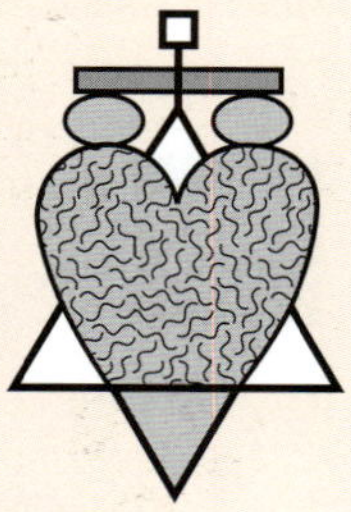

Test Figure

b has a larger Rectangle and the two Triangles should be White (see-through).

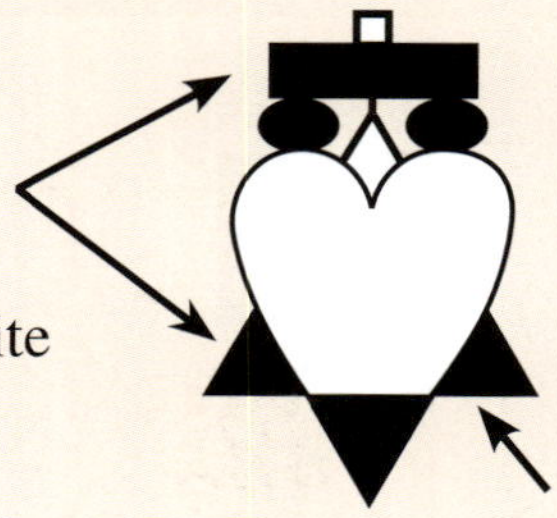

b

The Triangles in **d** are positioned higher on the silhouette than on the Test Figure.

d

Step 2 - Now look for silhouettes that have the same outline as the Test Figure but look for variations in the fills.

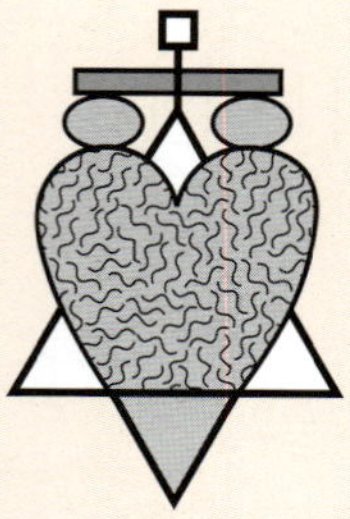

Test Figure

a has the correct outline but this Rectangle should have a Black Fill.

a

c matches the outline of the Test Figure and has the correct fills.

c

c is the silhouette of the Test Figure.

Exercise 23: 2

Which figure on the right is a silhouette of the Test Figure?

1)

Test Figure a b c d

Answer d

2)

Test Figure a b c d

Answer c

3)

Test Figure a b c d

Answer a

4)

Test Figure a b c d

Answer b

5)

Test Figure a b c d

Answer ____

The answer is c.

6)

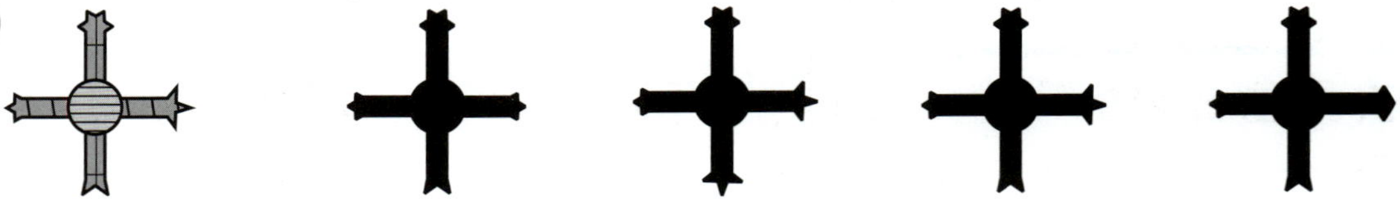

Test Figure a b c d

Answer c

7)

Test Figure a b c d

Answer d

8)

Test Figure a b c d

Answer a

9)

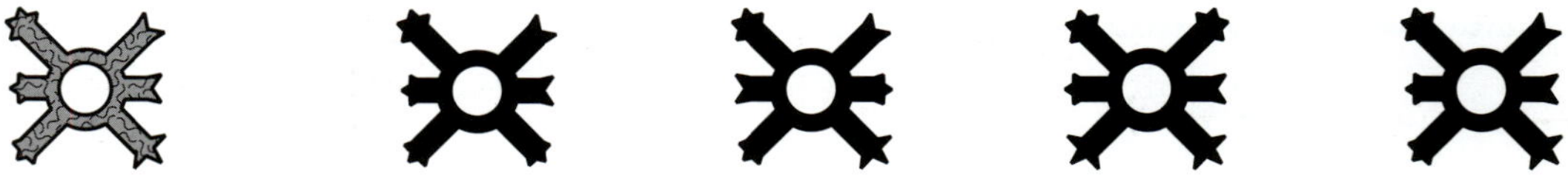

Test Figure a b c d

Answer a

10)

Test Figure a b c d

Answer c

Score

3. Silhouette Type 2

A **Silhouette Type 2** question is very similar to a Silhouette Type 1 question, except all areas of the figure that are not White receive a White Fill. White Fills of the silhouette are still regarded as see-through and therefore the Grey background can be seen.

Example: Which silhouette figure on the right matches the Test Figure?

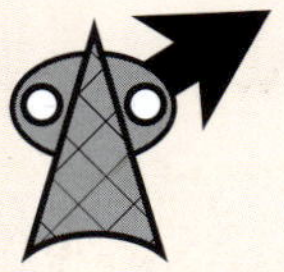

Test Figure

a

b

c

d

Step 1 - Look for any silhouettes that obviously do not match the outline of the Test Figure.

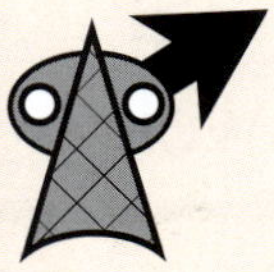

Test Figure

Both **a** and **c** have no see-through Circles, but the Test Figure has two White (see-through) Circles. Both **a** and **c** are incorrect.

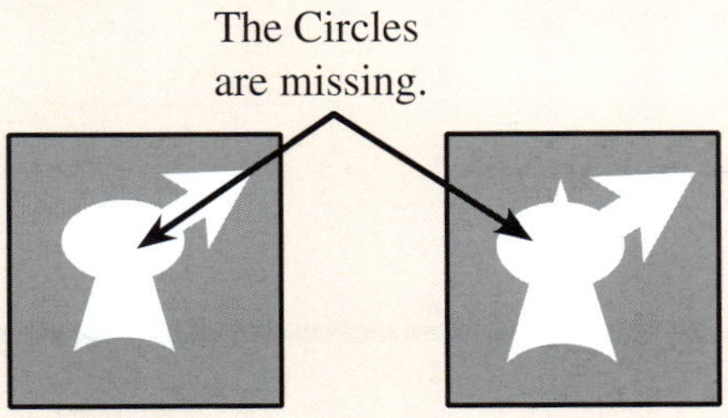

a **c**

Step 2 - Now look for more subtle differences between the silhouettes and the Test Figure.

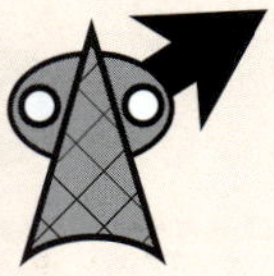

Test Figure

d does have the two see-through Circles and is almost entirely correct. However, there should be a small point at the top which is missing in **d**. This means **d** is incorrect.

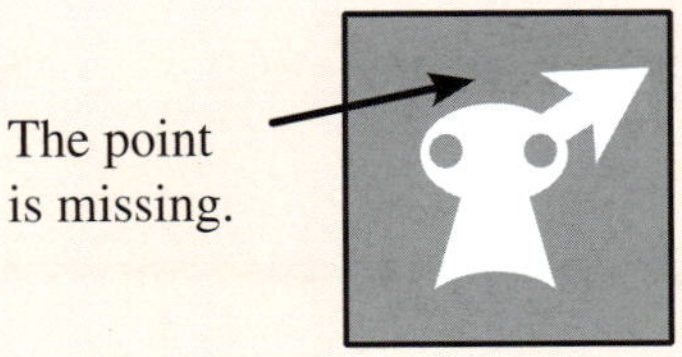

d

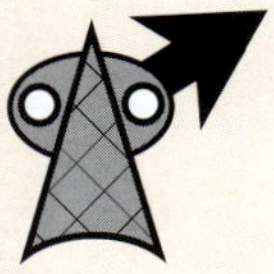

Test Figure

b

Compare the outline of **b** with the Test Figure. It matches it exactly. Silhouette **b** is the correct answer.

Exercise 23: 3

Which figure on the right is a silhouette of the Test Figure?

1)

Test Figure a b c d

Answer b

2)

Test Figure a b c d

Answer a

3)

Test Figure a b c d

Answer a

4)

Test Figure a b c d

Answer c

5)

Test Figure a b c d

Answer c

6)

Test Figure a b c d

Answer D

7)

Test Figure a b c d

Answer a

8)

Test Figure a b c d

Answer a

9)

Test Figure a b c d

Answer b

10)

Test Figure a b c d

Answer d

Score

4. Reverse Fills

A **Reverse Fill** question only uses Black and White Fills. Every area of a figure with a White Fill is reversed to a Black Fill, and every area with a Black Fill is reversed to a White Fill.

Example: Which figure on the right has reverse fills of the Test Figure?

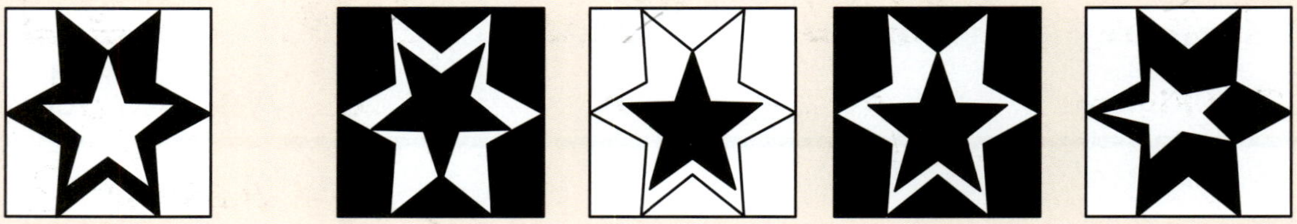

Test Figure **a** **b** **c** **d**

Step 1 - Look for any reverse fill figures where shapes have been changed or positioned incorrectly in the figure and do not match the Test Figure.

Test Figure

In **a** the enclosed Star in the middle of the figure is upside down.

a

In **d** the enclosed Star in the middle has been squashed and rotated.

d

Step 2 - Now check the fills have been correctly reversed on the remaining figures.

Test Figure

In **b** the outer fill has not been reversed. It should have a Black, not White, Fill.

b

c has all the correct shapes and all the fills have been reversed.

c

All the fills of the Test Figure have been reversed in **c**.

Exercise 23: 4

Which figure on the right has reverse fills of the Test Figure?

1)

Test Figure | a | b | c | d

Answer a

2)

Test Figure | a | b | c | d

Answer b

3)

Test Figure | a | b | c | d

Answer a

4)

Test Figure | a | b | c | d

Answer d

5)

Test Figure | a | b | c | d

Answer d

6)

Test Figure a b c d

Answer c

7)

Test Figure a b c d

Answer c

8)

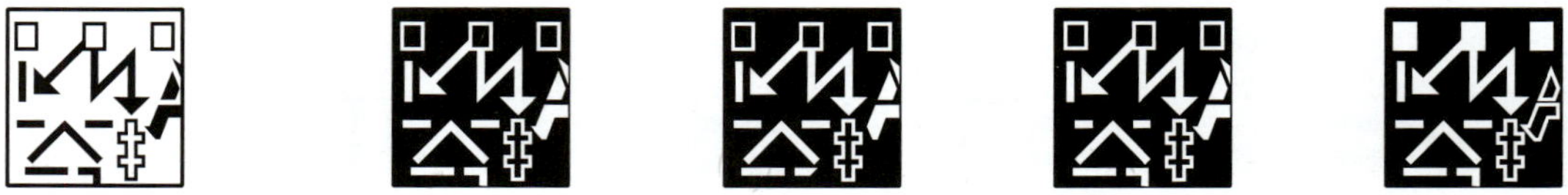

Test Figure a b c d

Answer a

9)

Test Figure a b c d

Answer b

10)

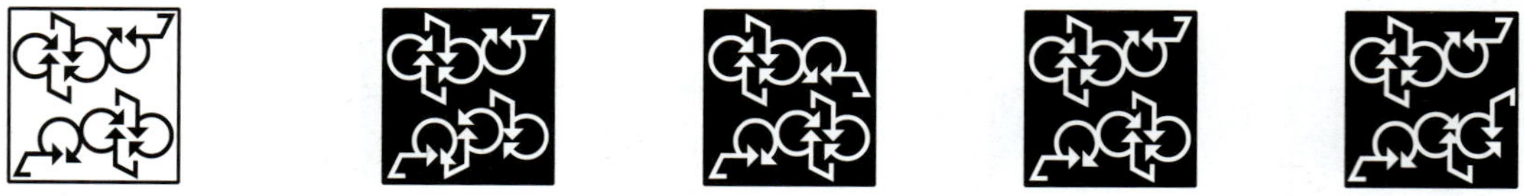

Test Figure a b c d

Answer c

Score

5. Jigsaw Type 1

Jigsaw questions involve identifying which jigsaw piece fits exactly inside the Test Figure. They are very similar to Replica Figures questions except they involve matching a White Fill jigsaw piece with a Grey Fill jigsaw piece.

Example: Which jigsaw piece on the right matches the Test Figure?

Test Figure **a** **b** **c** **d**

For the purpose of elimination it is best to focus on different parts of the jigsaw options in order to compare them with the Test Figure.

Step 1 - If we focus on the top half of the Test Figure we can immediately eliminate **a** and **c**.

Test Figure

In **a** one part of the shape has been altered.

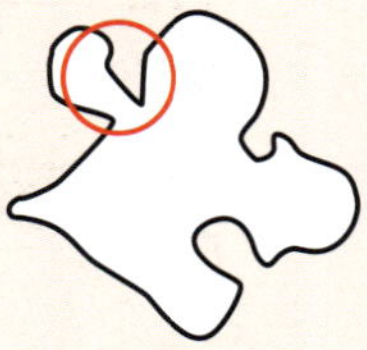

a

In **c** two parts of the shape have been altered.

c

Step 2 - If we focus on the bottom half of the Test Figure, **d** can be eliminated.

Test Figure

In **d** one part of the shape has been altered.

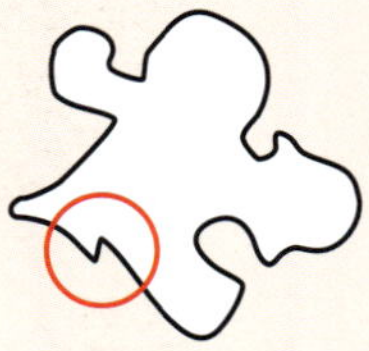

d

b is the correct answer. It matches the Test Figure exactly.

b

b is the correct jigsaw piece.

Exercise 23: 5

Which jigsaw piece matches the Test Figure?

1)

Test Figure   a   b   c   d

Answer a

2)

Test Figure   a   b   c   d

Answer b

3)

Test Figure   a   b   c   d

Answer a

4)

Test Figure   a   b   c   d

Answer c

5)

Test Figure   a   b   c   d

Answer b

6)

Test Figure a b c d

Answer ____

7)

Test Figure a b c d

Answer ____

8)

Test Figure a b c d

Answer ____

9)

Test Figure a b c d

Answer ____

10)

Test Figure a b c d

Answer ____

Score

6. Jigsaw Type 2

A variation on the Jigsaw question involves identifying how one jigsaw piece fits with another. This replicates the solving of a jigsaw puzzle in real life, with which we are all familiar.

Example: Which jigsaw piece on the right fits together with the Test Figure? Do not rotate either piece.

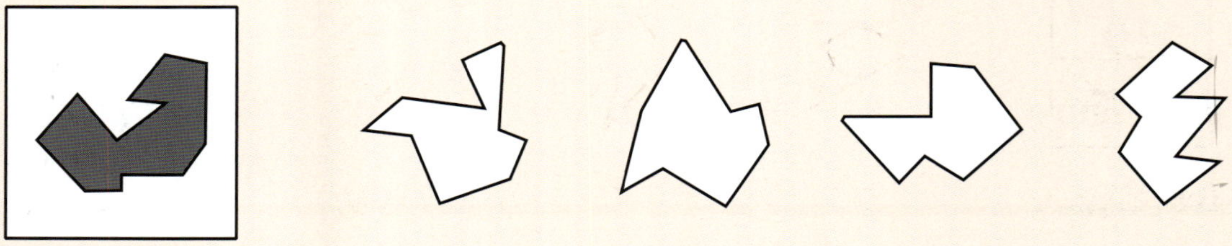

Test Figure **a** **b** **c** **d**

Step 1 - Look for any jigsaw pieces which are very different and could never be positioned around the Test Figure.

Test Figure

a is very different and it cannot fit with the Test Figure.

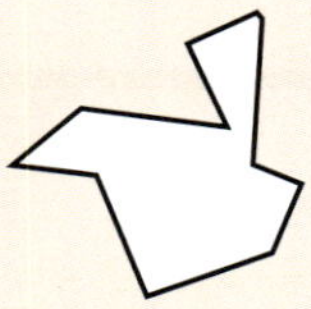

a

c also has no edges that could fit with the Test Figure.

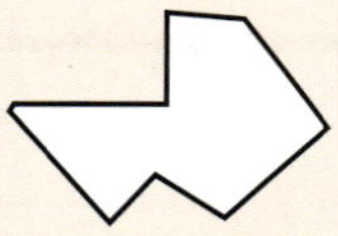

c

Step 2 - Now compare the two remaining options in order to eliminate the one that almost fits the Test Figure. Position each figure around the Test Figure to assess each possible join.

Test Figure

b has edges that almost fit with the Test Figure.

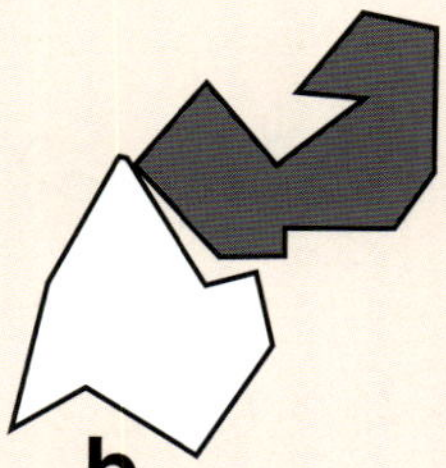

b

d is the correct answer as it exactly fits together with the Test Figure.

d

d is the jigsaw piece which fits with the Test Figure.

Exercise 23: 6

Which piece fits together with the Test Figure? Do not rotate either of them.

1)

Test Figure a b c d

Answer d

2)

Test Figure a b c d

Answer c

3)

Test Figure a b c d

Answer a

4)

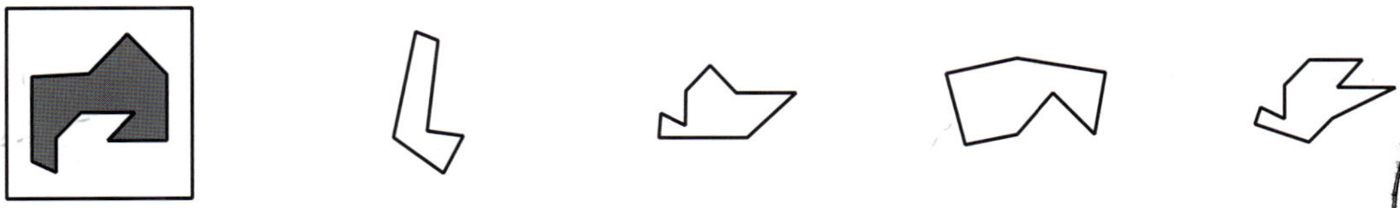

Test Figure a b c d

Answer d

5)

Test Figure a b c d

Answer b

6)

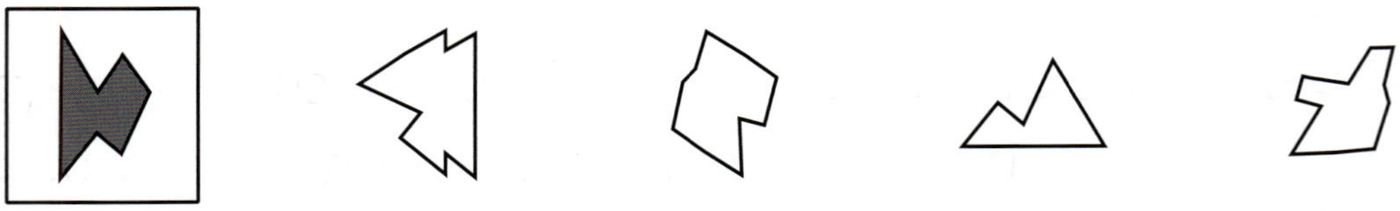

Test Figure a b c d

Answer c

7)

Test Figure a b c d

Answer b

8)

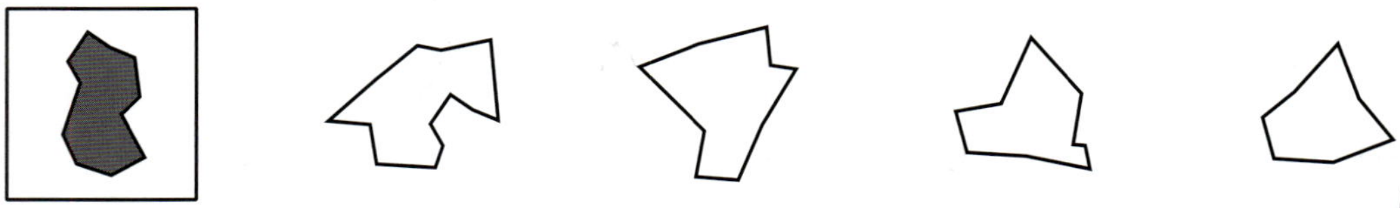

Test Figure a b c d

Answer d

9)

Test Figure a b c d

Answer ~~d~~ b

10)

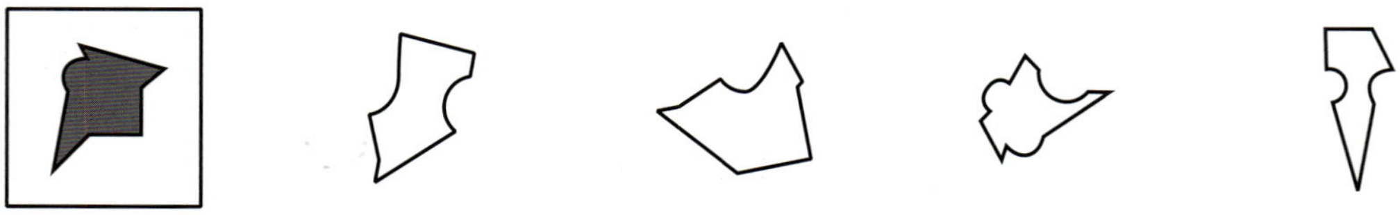

Test Figure a b c d

Answer b

Score

7. Hidden Figure

Hidden Figure questions involve finding a shape or figure when it has been carefully concealed within a larger figure. The shape or figure may have been rotated.

Example: Identify the figure on the right in which the Test Figure is hidden.

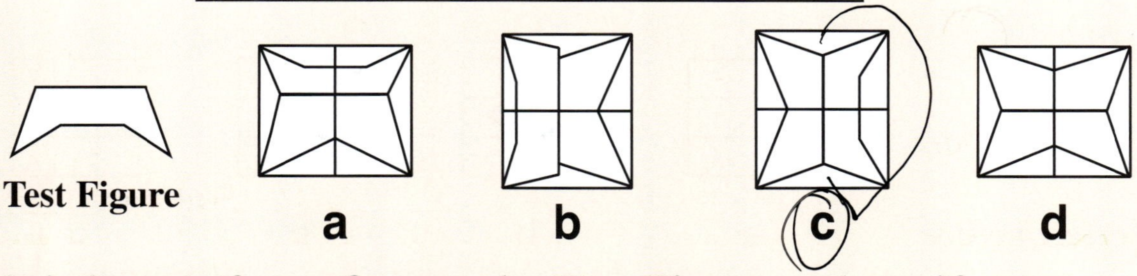

Test Figure — **a** — **b** — **c** — **d**

It is best to focus first on the Test Figure and see if you can visualise or recognise it in any other position.

Step 1 - Look initially for figures that can be easily eliminated. If we compare the Test Figure with **b** and **d** there are significant differences.

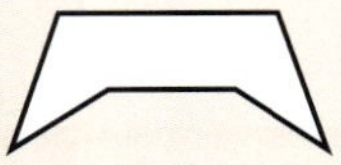

Test Figure

The Test Figure is not concealed in either **b** or **d**.

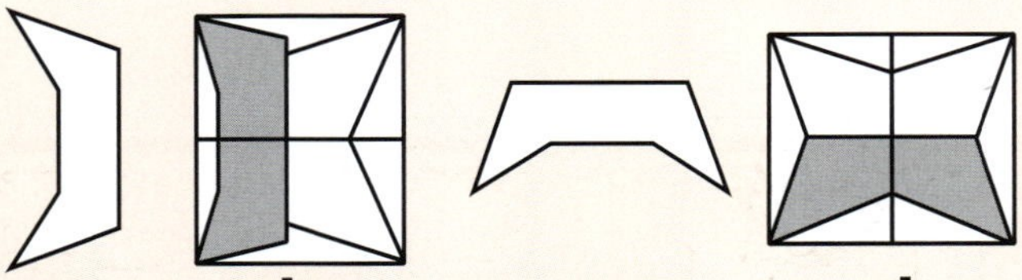

Test Figure **b** **Test Figure** **d**

Step 2 - Now examine the other alternatives more closely.

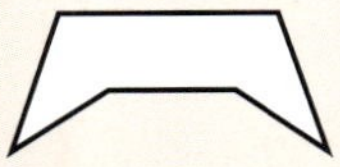

Test Figure

If the Test Figure is compared with **a** it is clear that it is not hidden within the figure.

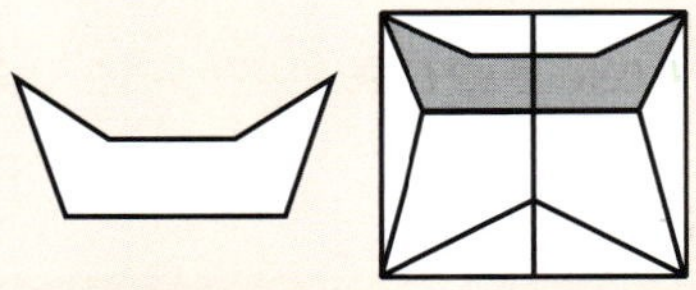

Test Figure **a**

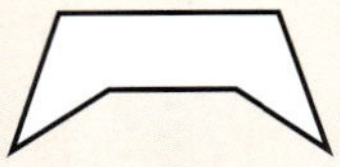

Test Figure

c must be the correct answer. If we compare the Test Figure with this figure it confirms that this is correct.

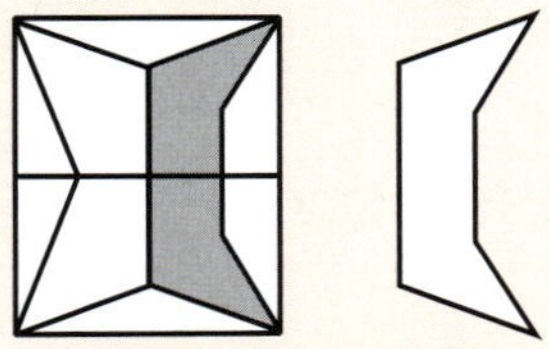

c **Test Figure**

The Test Figure is hidden within **c**.

Exercise 23: 7

Identify the figure on the right in which the Test Figure is hidden.

1)

Test Figure a b c d

Answer d

2)

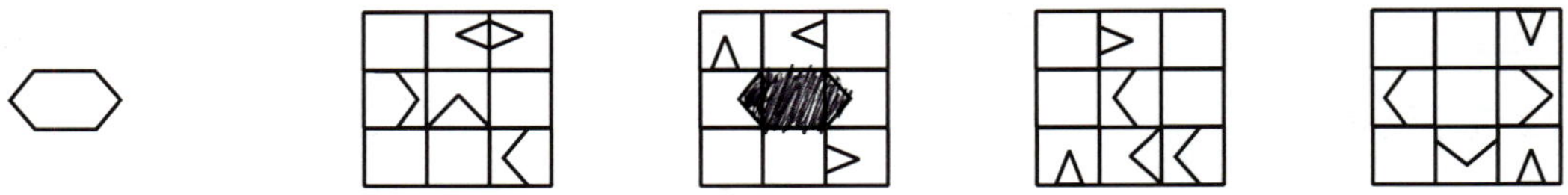

Test Figure a b c d

Answer b

3)

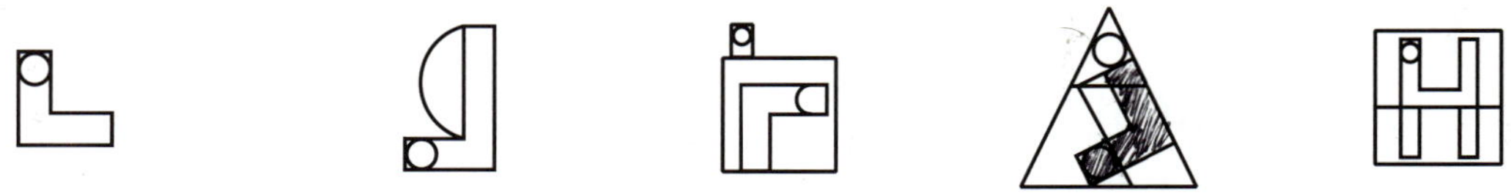

Test Figure a b c d

Answer c

4)

Test Figure a b c d

Answer a

5)

Test Figure a b c d

Answer b

6)

Test Figure **a** **b** **c** **d**

Answer c

7)

Test Figure **a** **b** **c** **d**

Answer d

8)

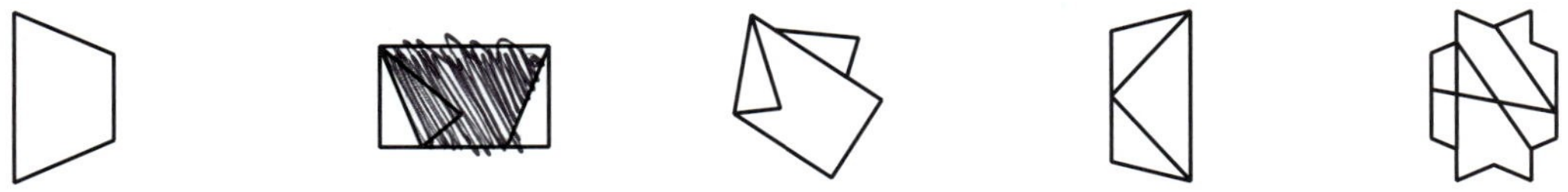

Test Figure **a** **b** **c** **d**

Answer a

9)

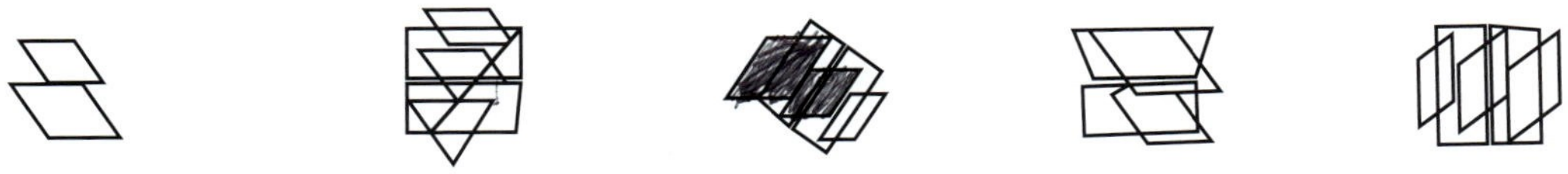

Test Figure **a** **b** **c** **d**

Answer b

10)

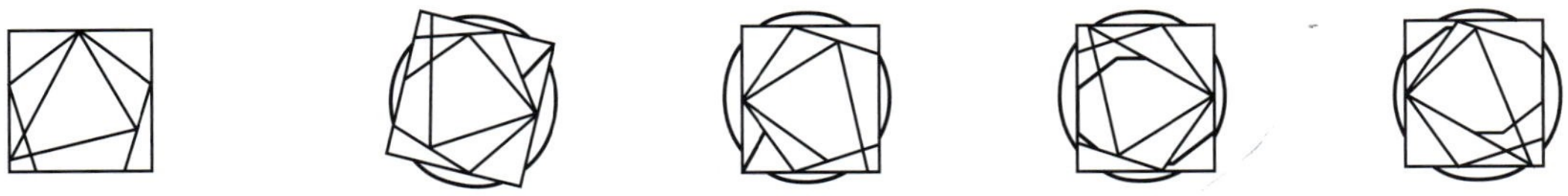

Test Figure **a** **b** **c** **d**

Answer a

Score

8. Hidden Pattern

A **Hidden Pattern** is similar to a Hidden Shape but is much more difficult to detect within a series of points on a grid.

Example: The figure on the left will fit the grid on the right in one position only. Draw the figure on the right-hand grid.

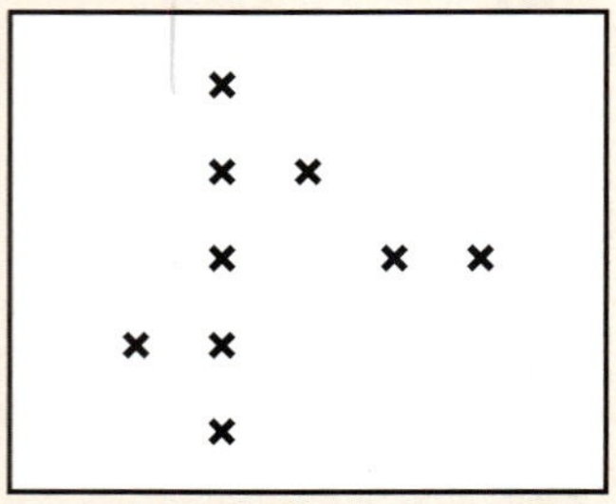

Test Figure

This figure is contained within the grid on the right.

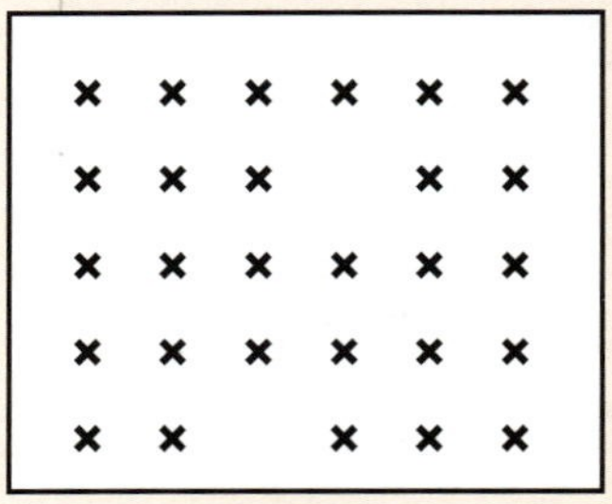

Grid

Step 1 - Draw the figure on the grid. There are two positions that can be easily eliminated.

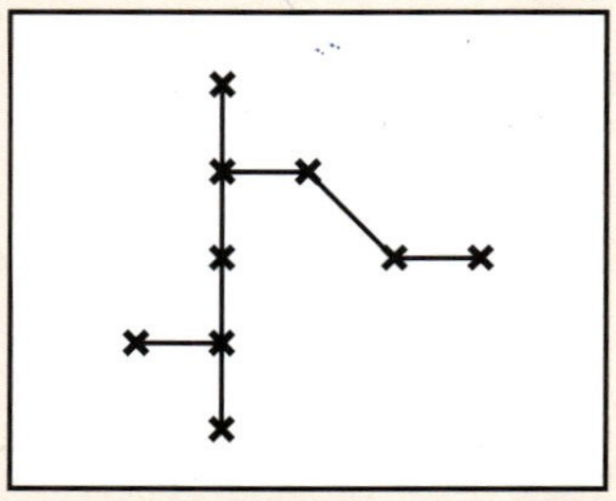

Test Figure

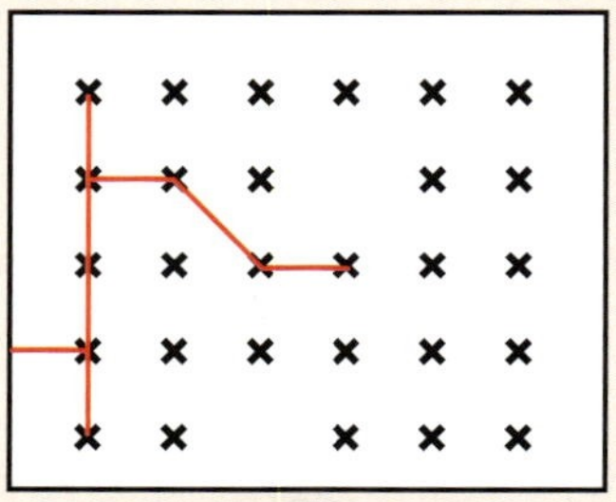

Position One

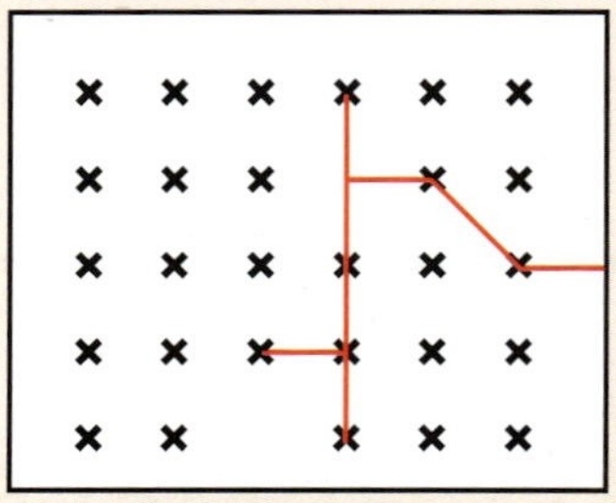

Position Two

The Test Figure does not fit either Position One or Position Two.

Step 2 - More likely positions can now be closely checked.

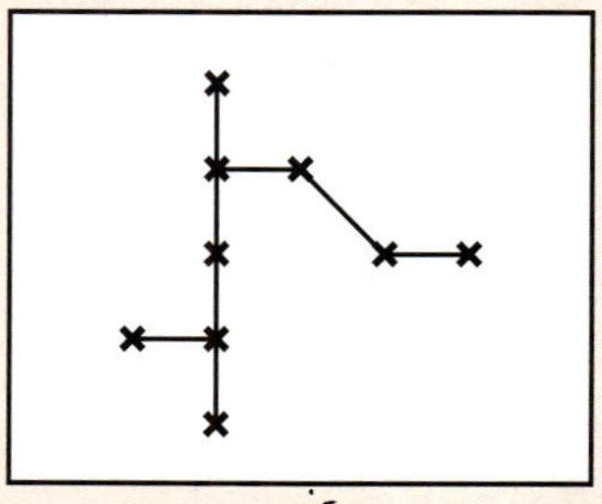

Test Figure

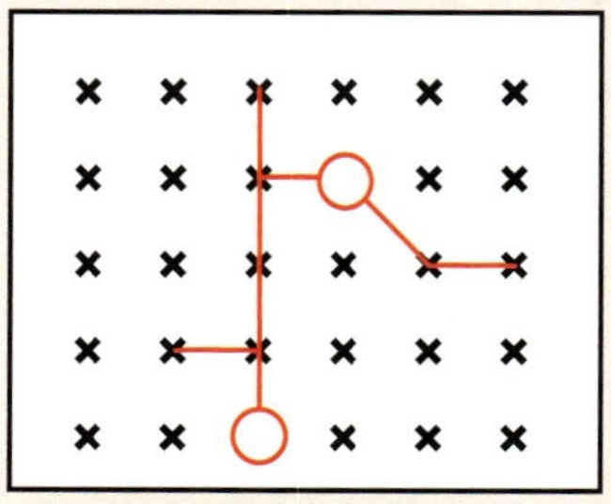

Position Three

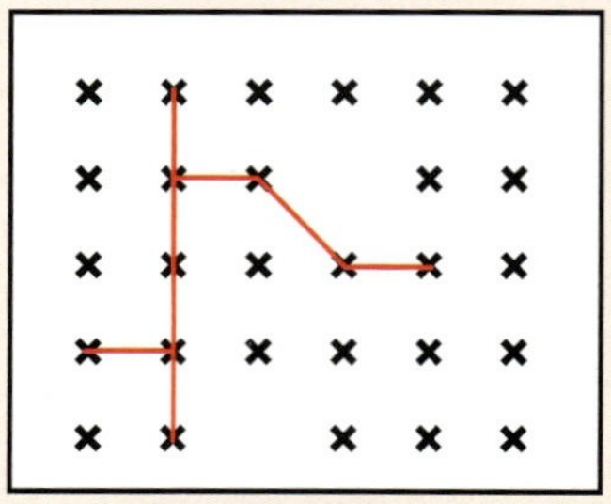

Position Four

The Test Figure almost fits in Position Three but the circles show where two Crosses are out of place. The Test Figure only works in Position Four.

The Test Figure matches Position Four.

Exercise 23: 8 Draw the Test Figure on the grid.

1)

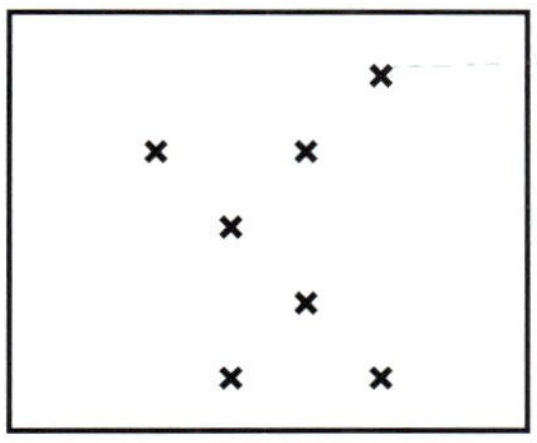
Test Figure

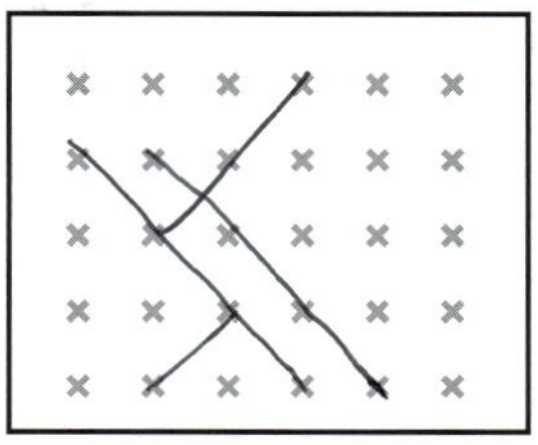
Working Out

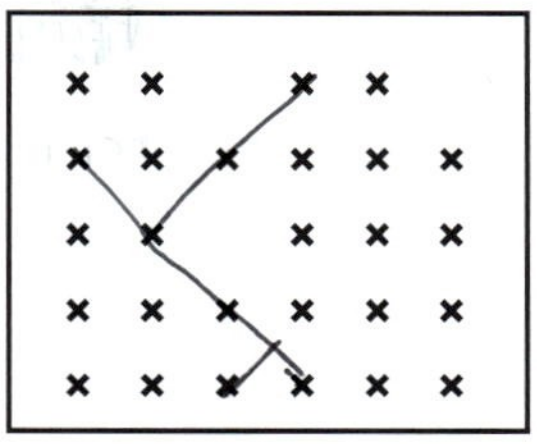
Answer

2)

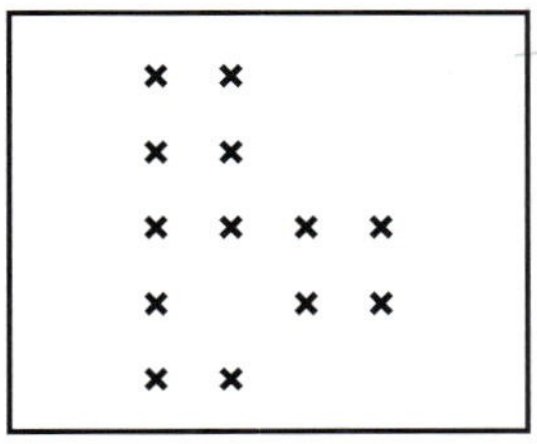
Test Figure

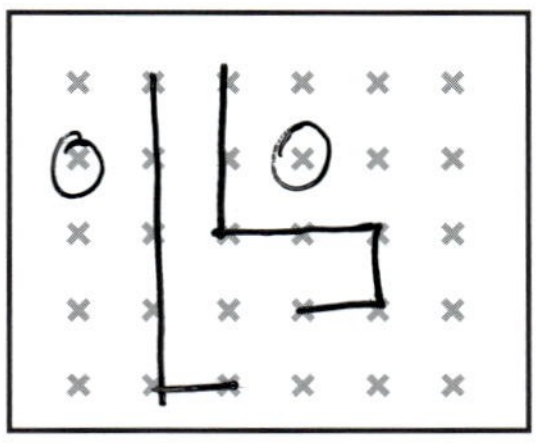
Working Out

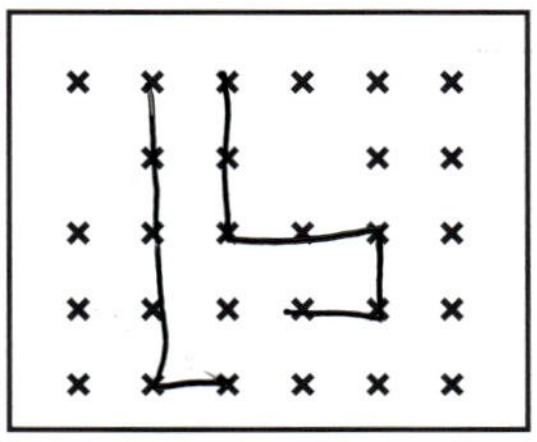
Answer

3)

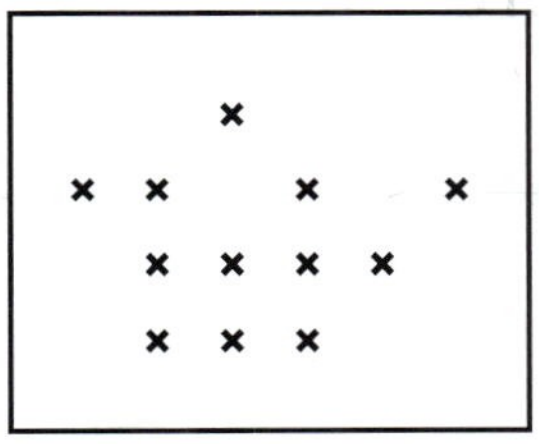
Test Figure

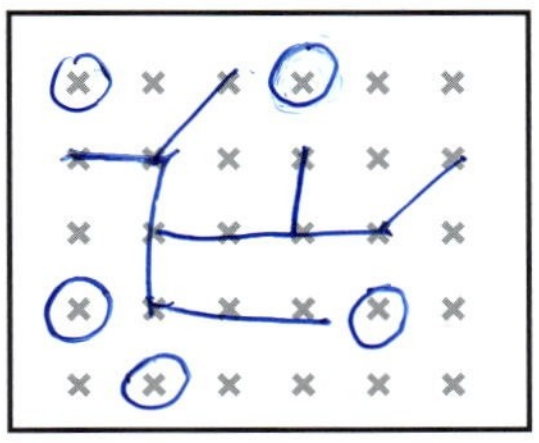
Working Out

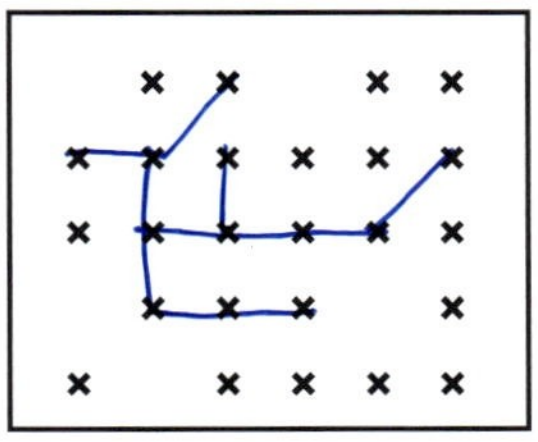
Answer

4)

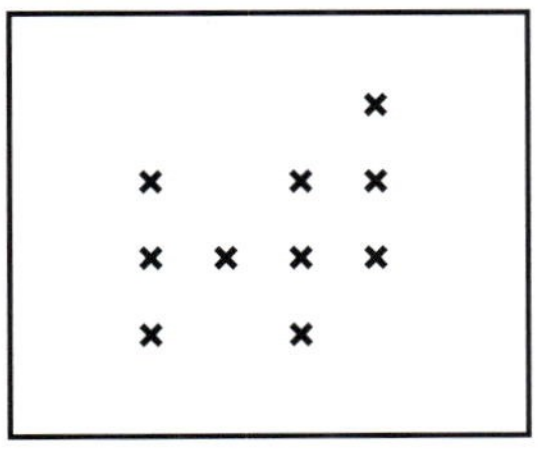
Test Figure

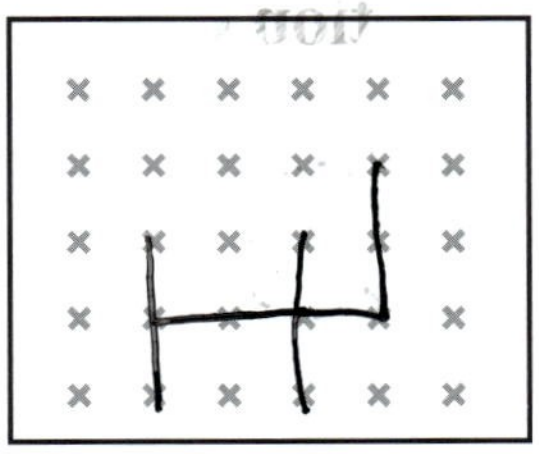
Working Out

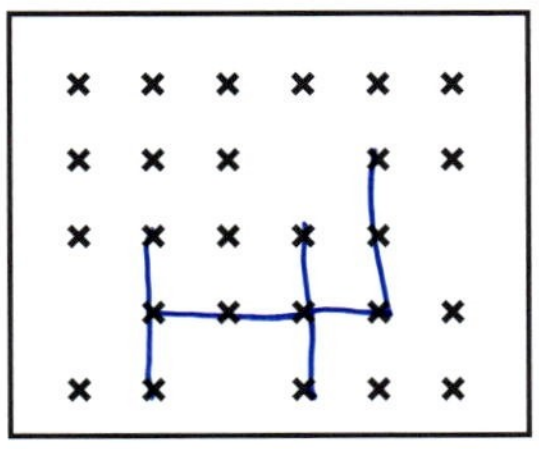
Answer

5)

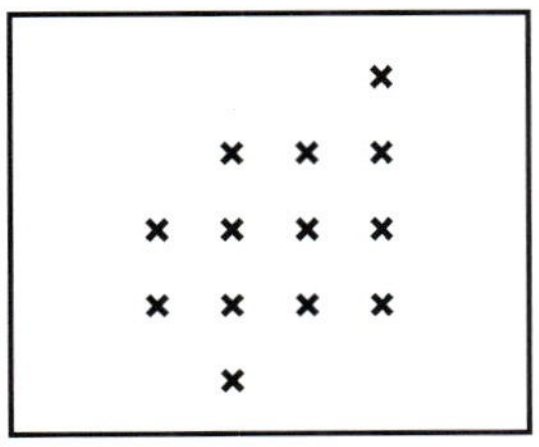
Test Figure

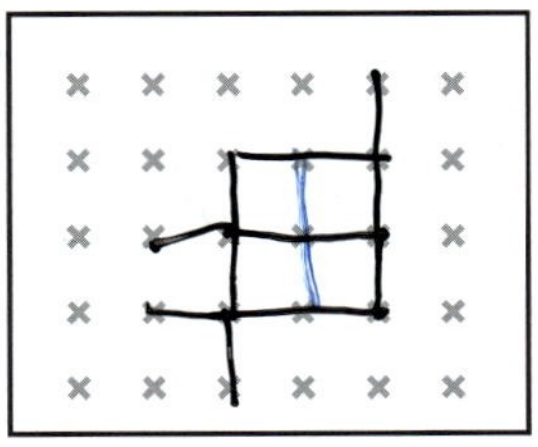
Working Out

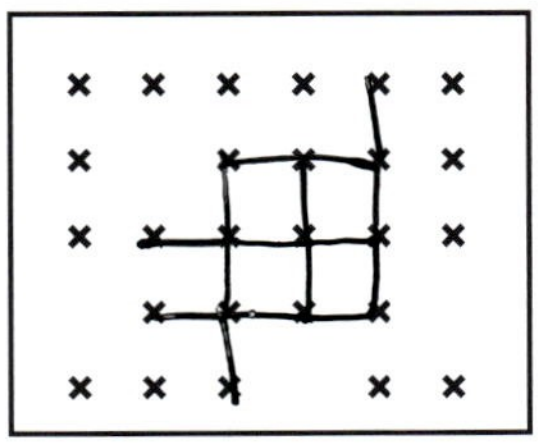
Answer

6)

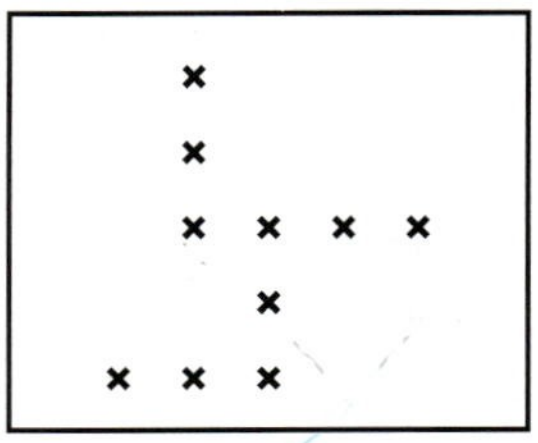

Test Figure

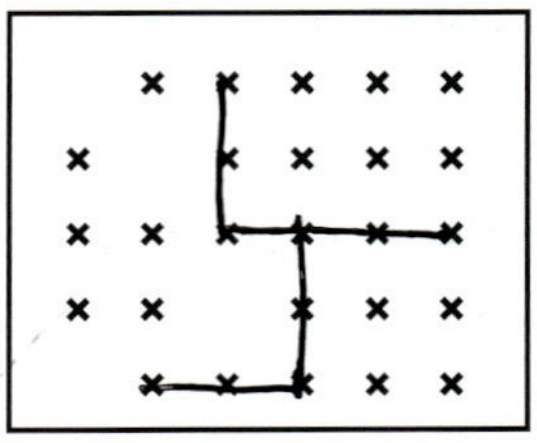

Answer

7)

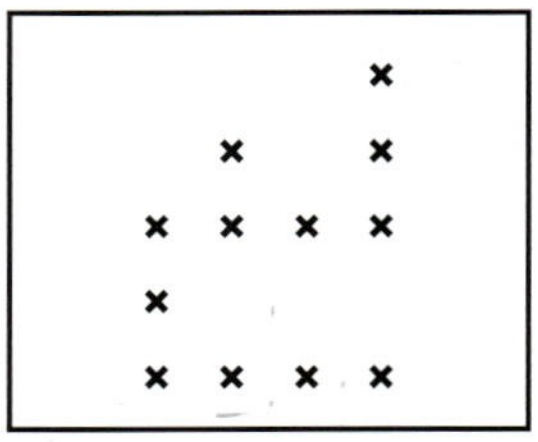

Test Figure

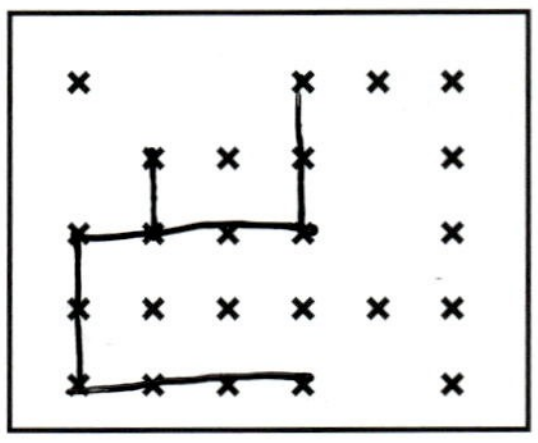

Answer

8)

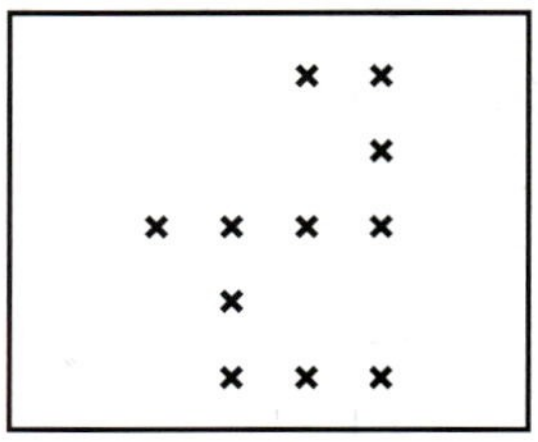

Test Figure

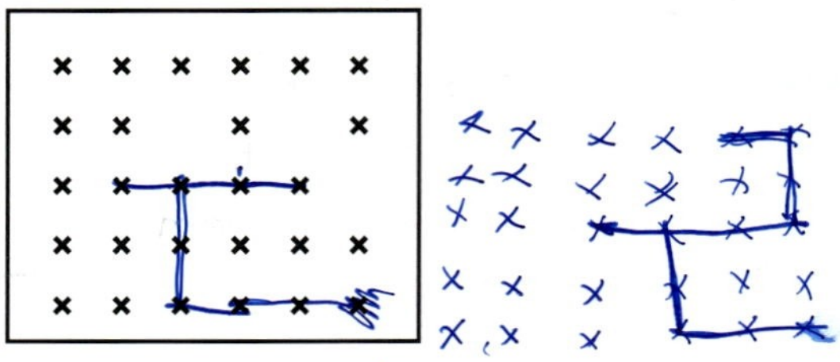

Answer

9)

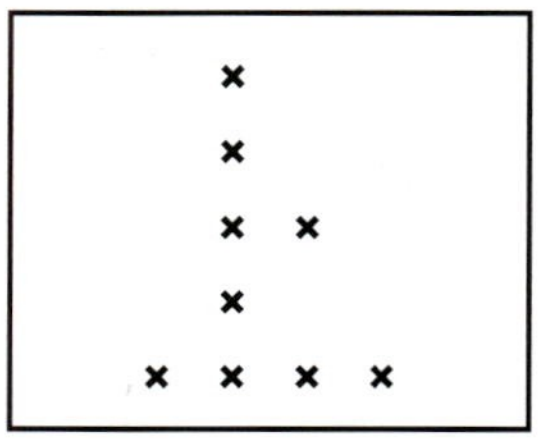

Test Figure

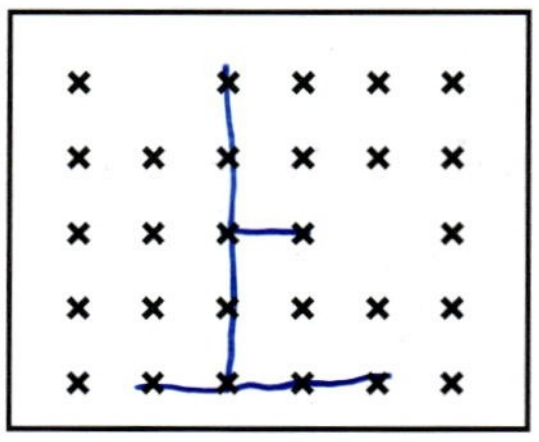

Answer

10)

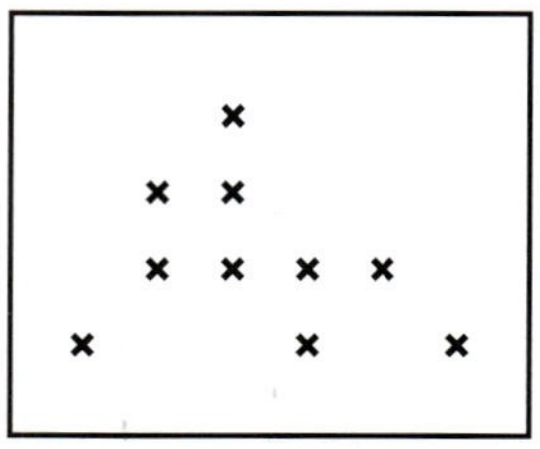

Test Figure

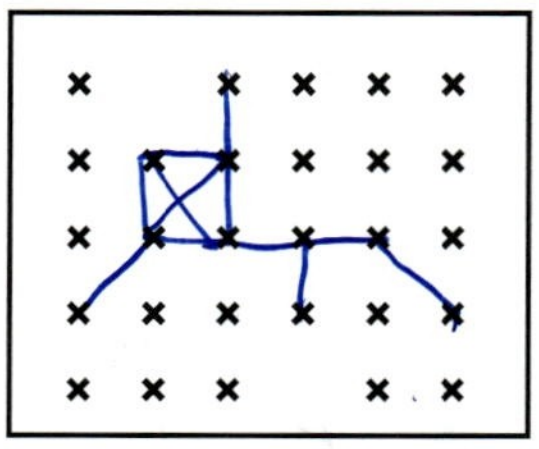

Answer

Score

9. Fitting Shapes Inside

Fitting Shapes Inside other shapes is similar to Jigsaw Type 1 as it involves imagining placing shapes within another shape.

Example: Three shapes will fit into the Test Shape without being rotated. Which shape is not required?

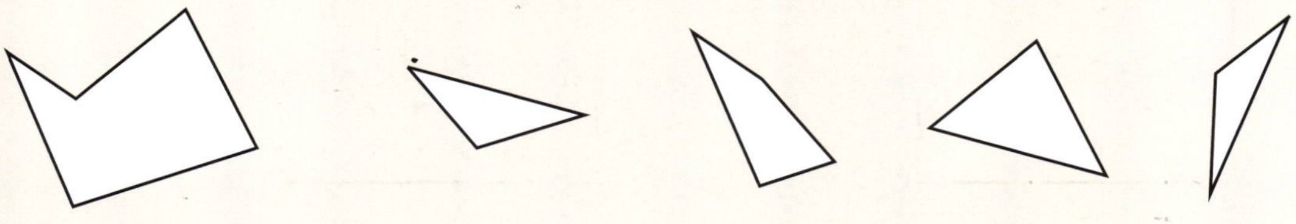

Test Shape   **a**   **b**   **c**   **d**

Step 1 - Look for one shape that fits easily into the Test Shape to begin with. **b** appears to do this.

Test Shape

b seems to fit into the left side of the Test Shape.

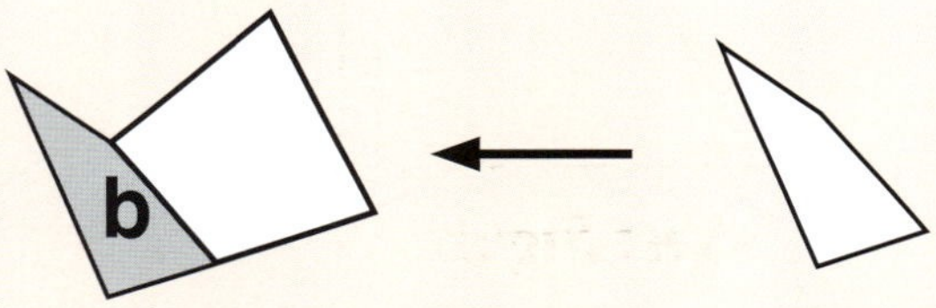

Test Shape   **b**

Step 2 - Once the first shape is in place it is easier to see which other shapes might fit. **a** is next.

Test Shape

a must be placed next to **b**.

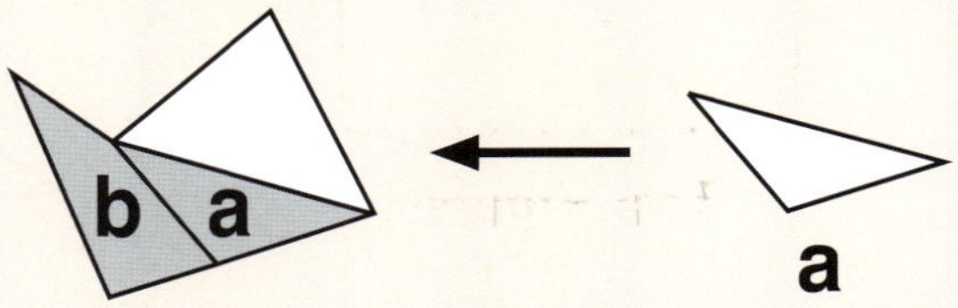

Test Shape   **a**

Step 3 - Only **c** will now fit.

Test Shape

c must be placed next to **b**.

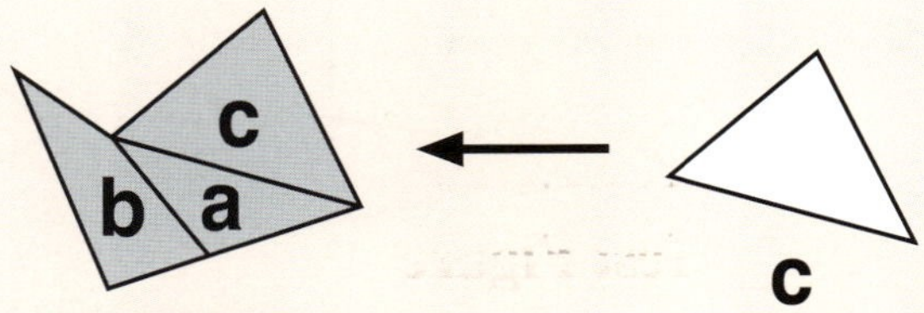

Test Shape   **c**

d will not fit into the Test Shape.

Exercise 23: 9

Three shapes will fit into the Test Shape without being rotated. Which shape is not required?

1)

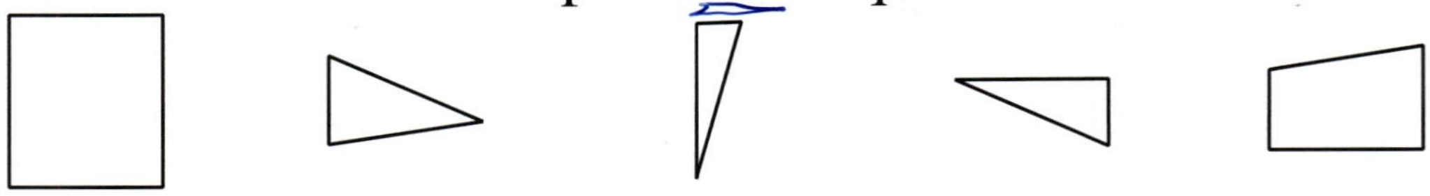

Test Shape **a** **b** **c** **d**

Answer ____

2)

Test Shape **a** **b** **c** **d**

Answer ____

3)

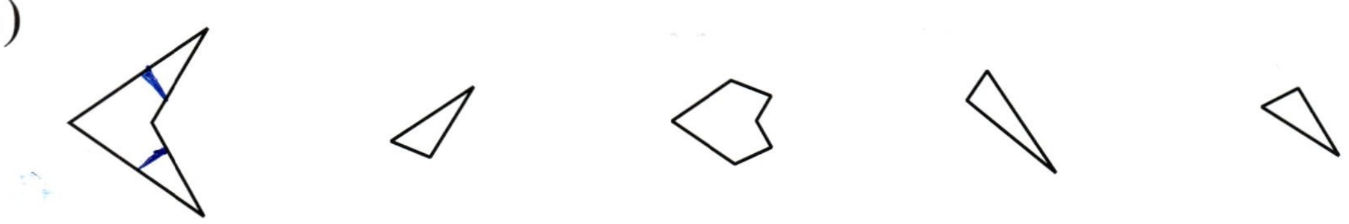

Test Shape **a** **b** **c** **d**

Answer ____

4)

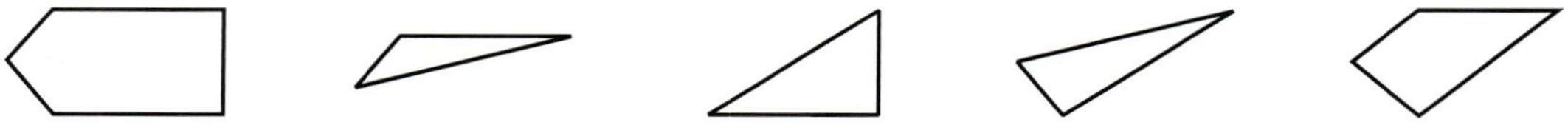

Test Shape **a** **b** **c** **d**

Answer ____

5)

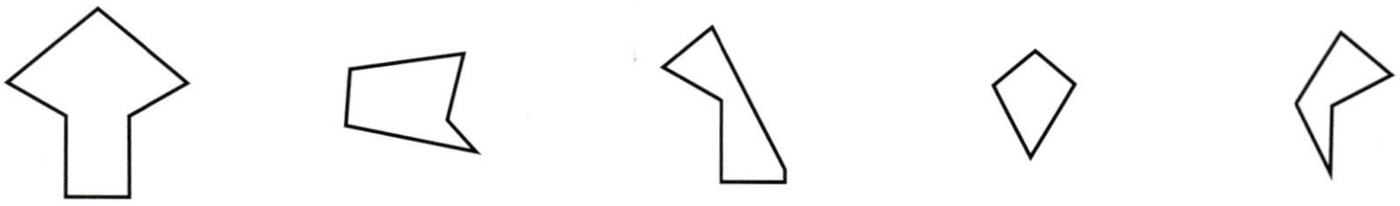

Test Shape **a** **b** **c** **d**

Answer ____

6)

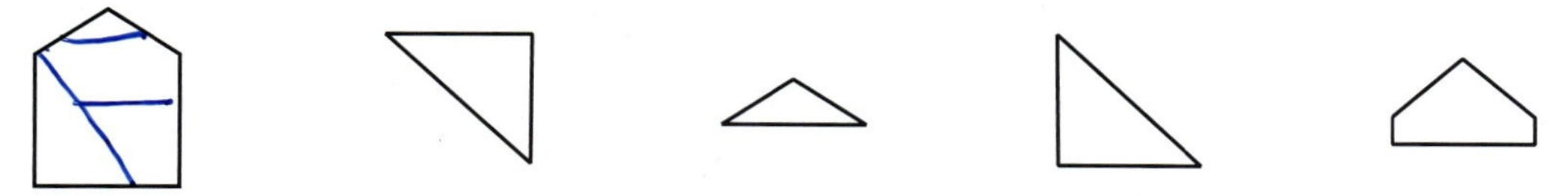

Test Shape **a** **b** **c** **d**

Answer d

7)

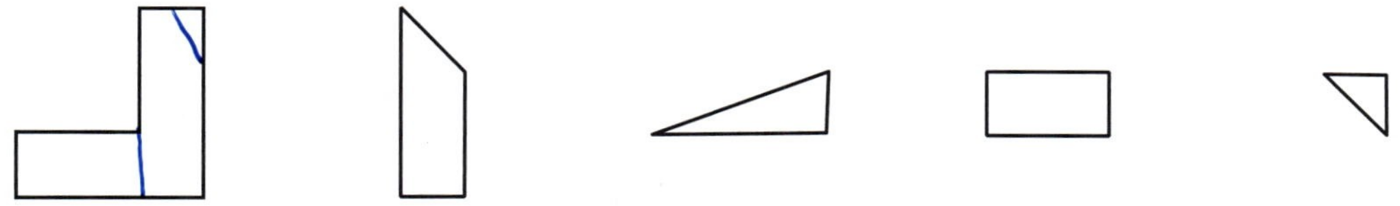

Test Shape **a** **b** **c** **d**

Answer b

8)

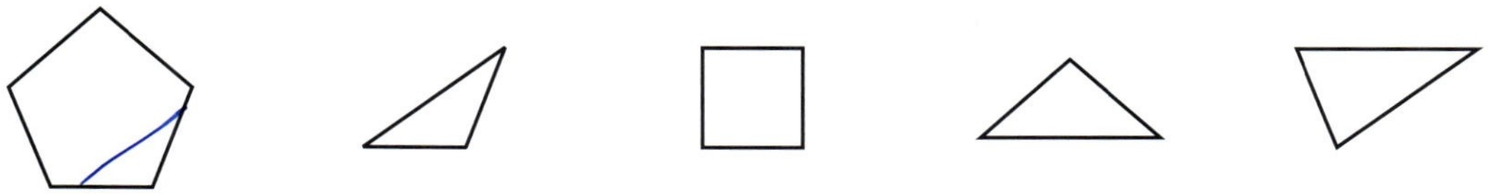

Test Shape **a** **b** **c** **d**

Answer a

9)

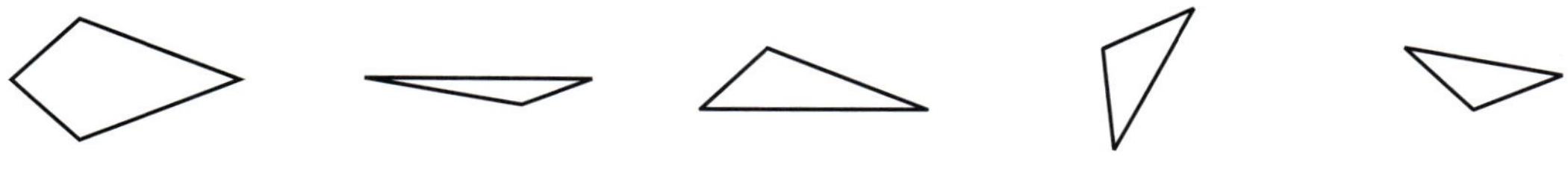

Test Shape **a** **b** **c** **d**

Answer c

10)

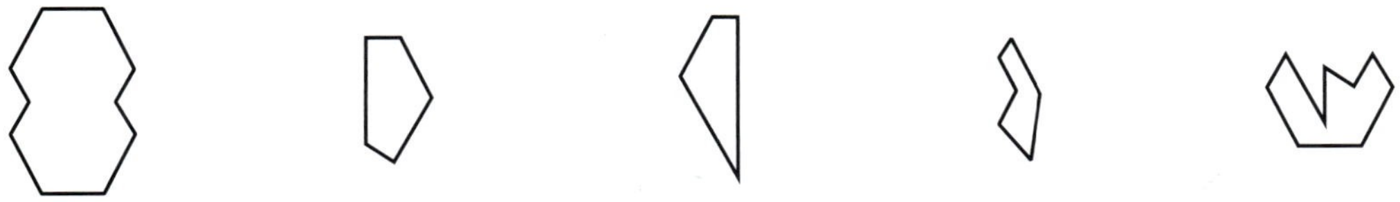

Test Shape **a** **b** **c** **d**

Answer d

Score

10. Assembling Figures

Assembling Figures is a variation on Fitting Shapes Inside and Jigsaw Type 2 and requires the same skills.

Example: Assemble the figure on the left by correctly rearranging the pieces to the right of the grid.

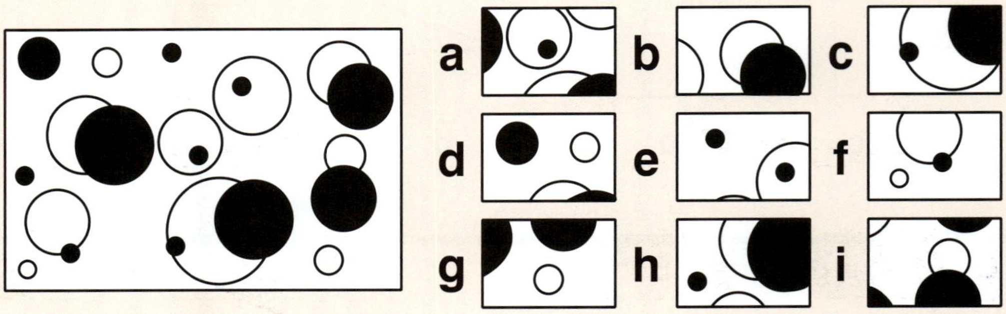

Step 1 - Look for the four corner pieces first as they have two outer edges meaning there is less material to match them against.

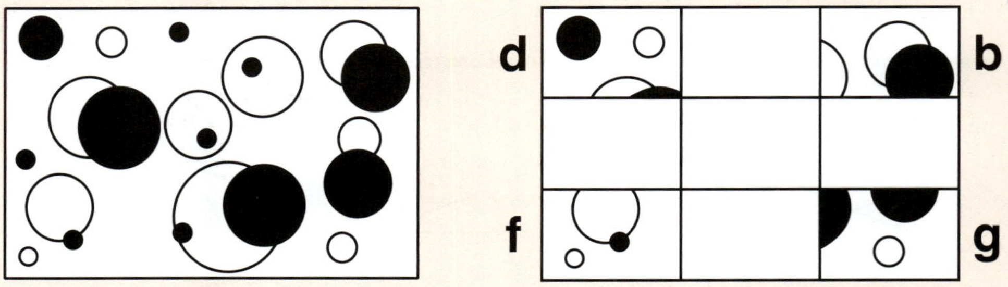

Step 2 - Now the other four edge pieces can be positioned as they can be matched against the corner pieces. Once completed the centre piece can be positioned.

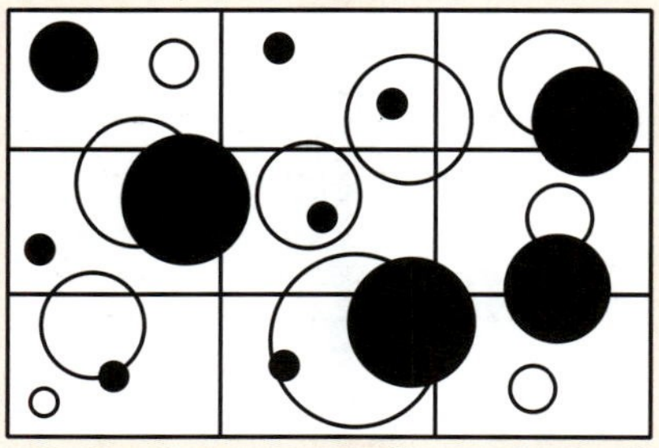

1. **d**	2. **e**	3. **b**
4. **h**	5. **a**	6. **i**
7. **f**	8. **c**	9. **g**

The assembled grid exactly matches the initial figure.

Exercise 23: 10

Assemble the figure. Complete the answer grids below.

1)

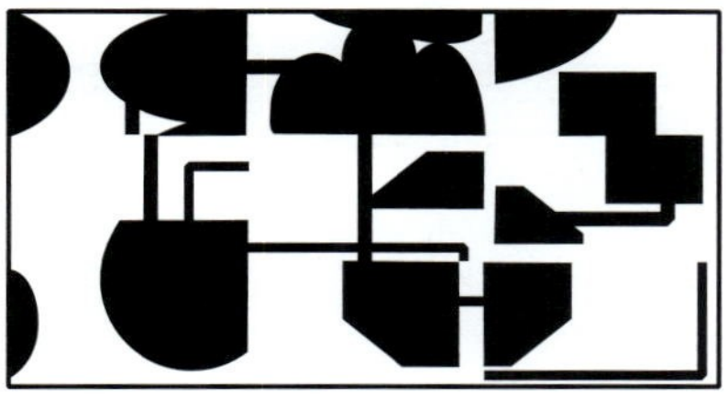

a  b 

c  d 

e  f 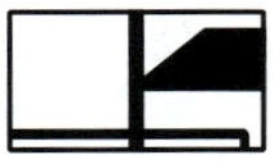

g  h 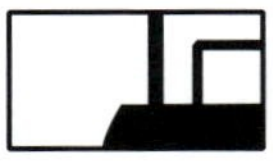

i 

2)

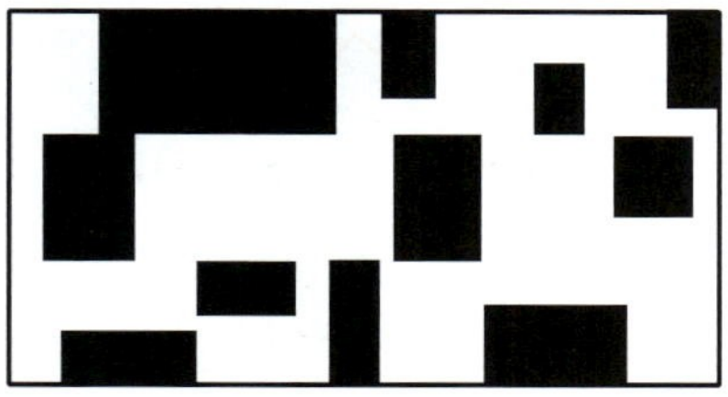

a  b 

c  d 

e  f 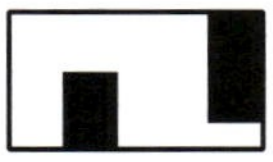

g  h 

i 

Each answer square corresponds with a piece of the figure.

1. C	2. F	3. a
4. h	5. G	6. d
7. e	8. i	9. b

1. d	2. g	3. f
4. c	5. e	6. b
7. i	8. f	9. a

3)

4)

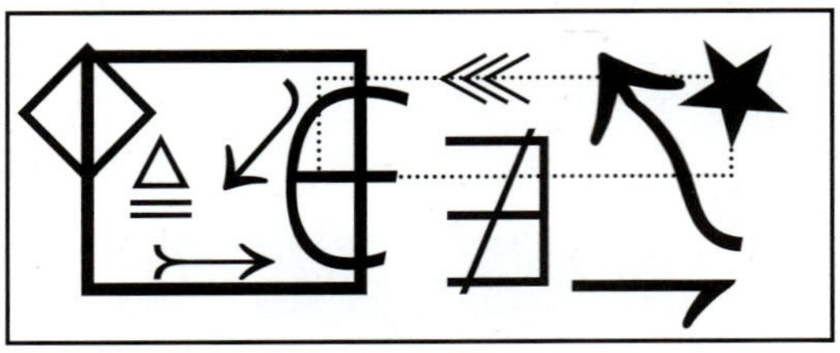

a  b 

c  d 

e  f 

g  h 

i 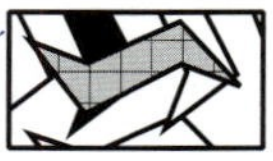

a  b 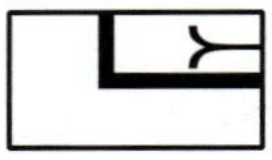

c 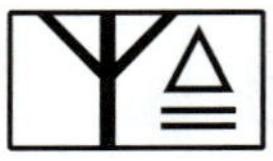 d 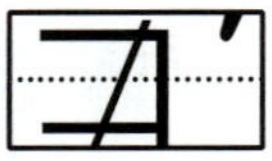

e  f 

g 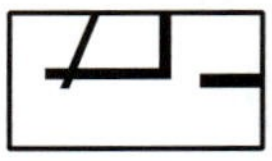 h 

i 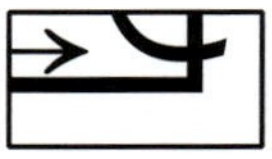 j 

k  l 

Each answer square corresponds with a piece of the figure.

1. e	2. a	3. b
4. f	5. d	6. g
7. h	8. i	9. c

1. H	2. f	3. a	4. E
5. C	6. L	7. d	8. K
9. b	10. i	11. g	12. J

5)

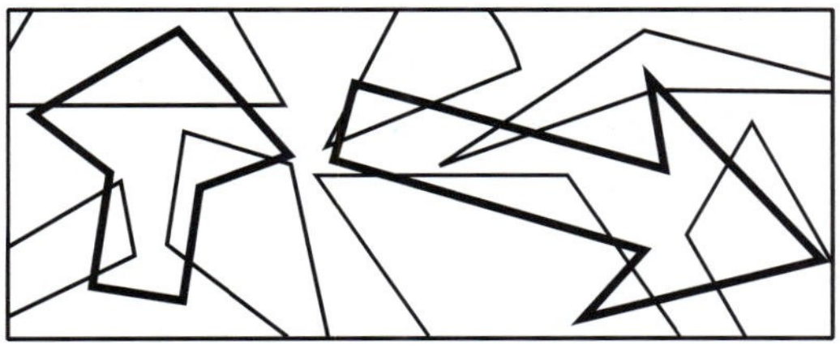

6)

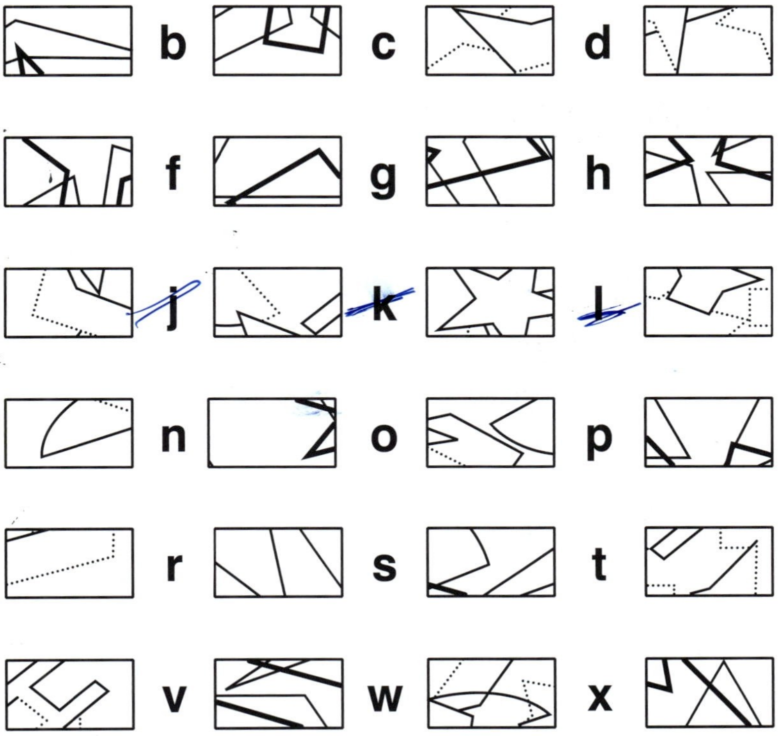

Each answer square corresponds with a piece of the figure.

1. ___	2. ___	3. ___	4. ___
5. ___	6. ___	7. ___	8. ___
9. ___	10. ___	11. ___	12. ___

1. k	2. ___	3. ___	4. u
5. i	6. ___	7. j	8. ___
9. M	10. ___	11. ___	12. q

7)

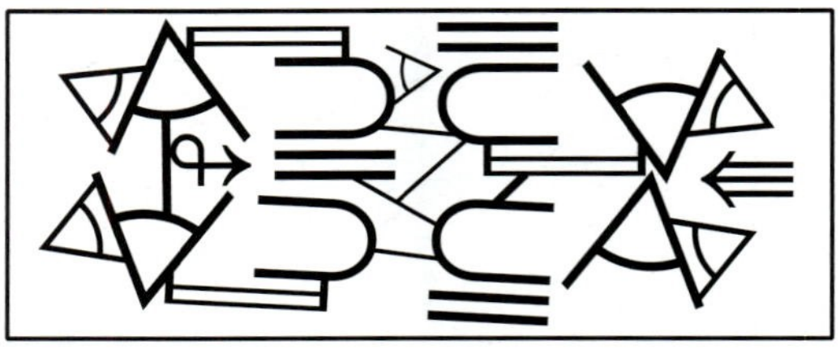

8)

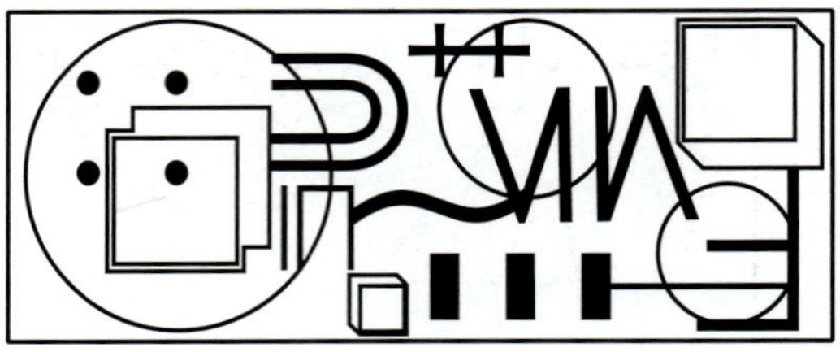

a  b 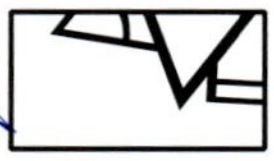

c  d 

e  f 

g  h 

i  j 

k  l 

a  b 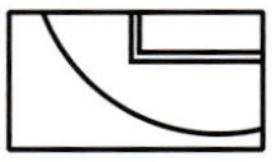

c  d 

e 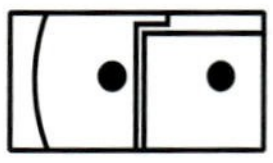 f 

g  h 

i 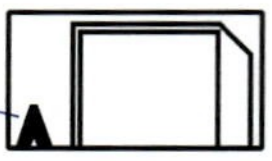 j 

k  l 

Each answer square corresponds with a piece of the figure.

1. e	2. [illegible]	3. d	4. G
5. b	6. j	7. c	8. a
9. f	10. h	11. i	12. K

1. j	2. h	3. d	4. i
5. e	6. c	7. g	8. a
9. b	10. L	11. F	12. K

9)

10)

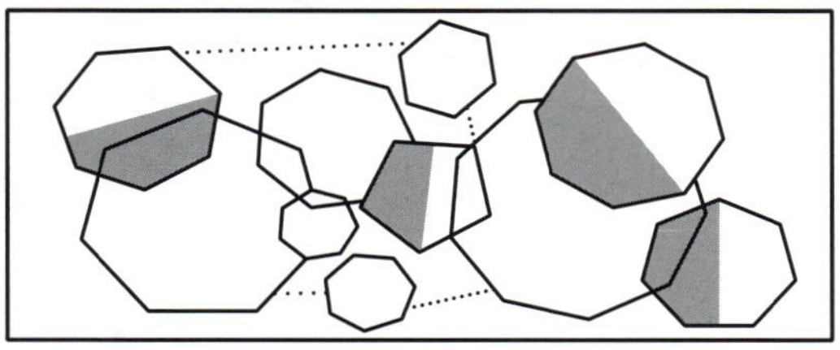

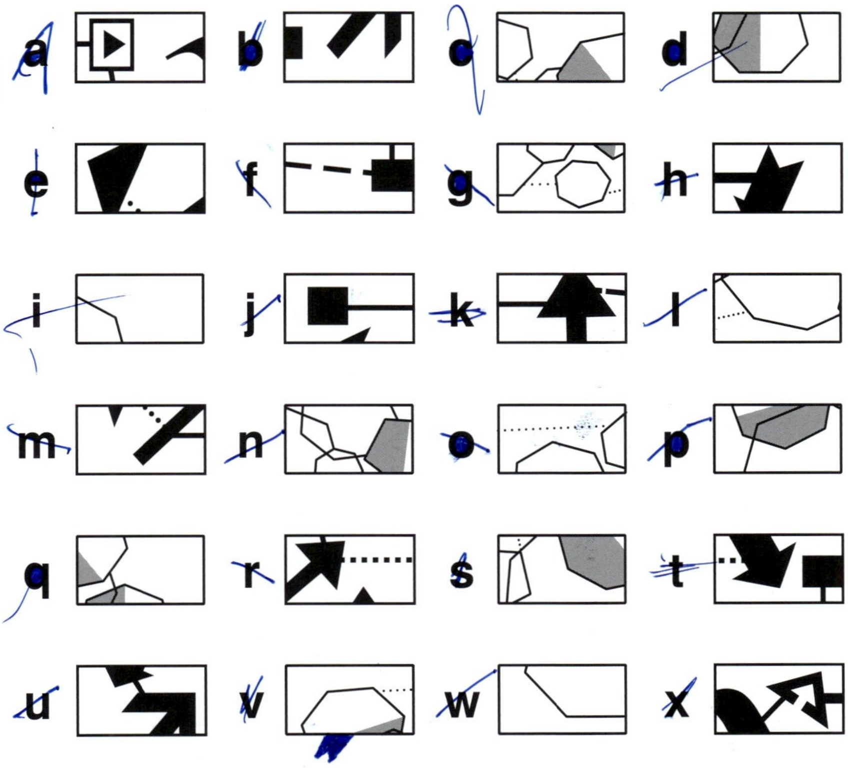

Each answer square corresponds with a piece of the figure.

1. ___	2. ___	3. ___	4. ___
5. ___	6. ___	7. ___	8. ___
9. ___	10. ___	11. ___	12. ___

1. ___	2. ___	3. ___	4. ___
5. ___	6. ___	7. ___	8. ___
9. ___	10. ___	11. ___	12. ___

Score

11. Adding Figures

Adding Figures is a variation on Assembling Figures, Fitting Shapes Inside and Jigsaw Type 2 and requires similar skills. When adding figures, Black Fills always override or replace Grey and White Fills.

Example: Which new figure is made when these two Test Figures are added together?

Test Figures **a** **b** **c** **d**

Step 1 - Try and eliminate the alternatives that have more obvious changes. **a** and **b** are very different from the original Test Figures.

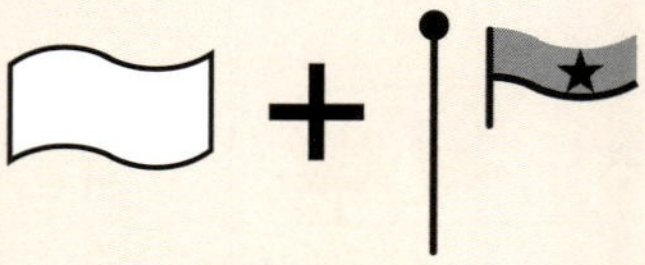

Test Figures

a has no White space between the flag and the flag pole.

a

In **b** the top of the flagpole should be Black.

b

Step 2 - **c** and **d** are very similar and need to be examined more closely.

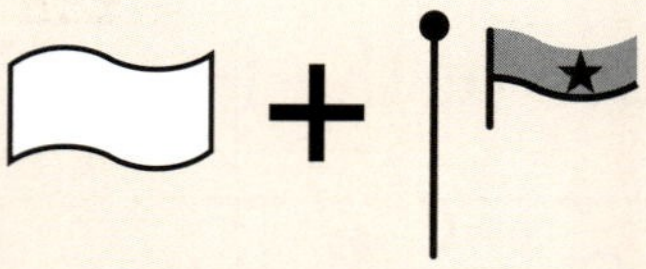

Test Figures

In **d** everything is correct except the Star on the Flag has been rotated by 180°.

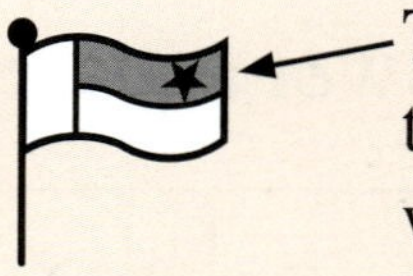

d

The Star is the wrong way up.

Step 3 - Now check **c** with the Test Figures to ensure it is the correct answer.

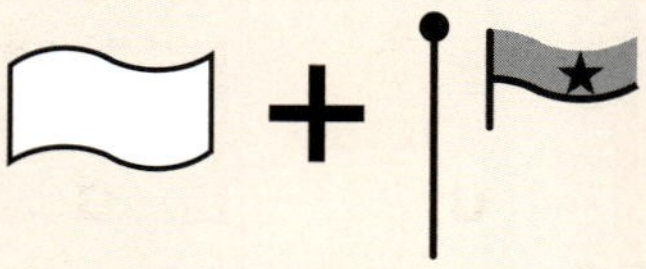

Test Figures

c

When the Test Figures are added together **c** will be the answer.

Exercise 23: 11

Which new figure is made when these two Test Figures are added together?

1)

Test Figures a b c d

Answer b

2)

Test Figures a b c d

Answer c

3)

Test Figures a b c d

Answer d

4)

Test Figures a b c d

Answer a

5)

Test Figures a b c d

Answer c

6)

Test Figures a b c d

Answer ____

7)

Test Figures a b c d

Answer ____

8)

Test Figures a b c d

Answer ____

9)

Test Figures a b c d

Answer ____

10)

Test Figures a b c d

Answer ____ **Score** 

12. Subtracting Figures

Subtracting Figures is the opposite of Adding Figures but still involves being able to recognise a shape or figure.

Example: Which figure remains after the second Test Figure has been subtracted from the first Test Figure?

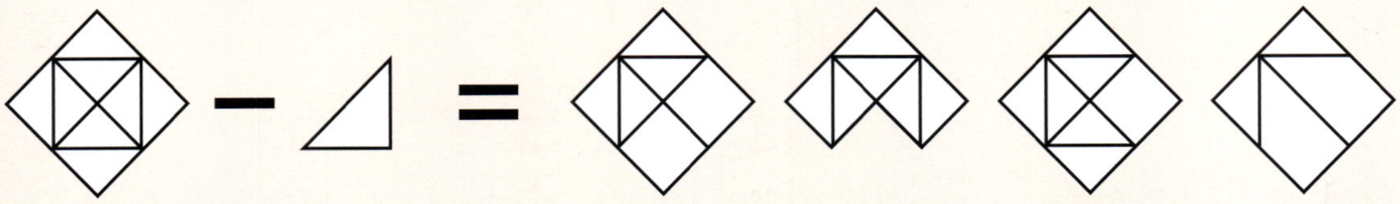

Test Figures a b c d

Step 1 - It is best to first eliminate the options that are obviously incorrect. **b** and **c** are very different from the original Test Figures.

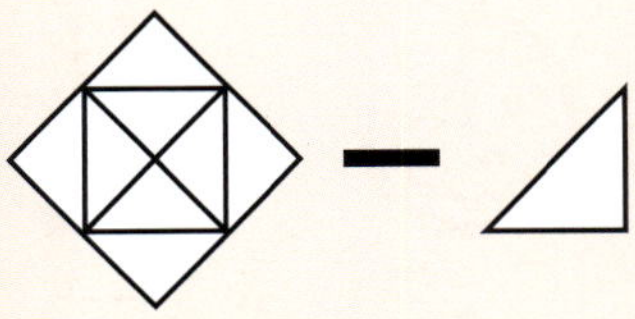

Test Figures

In **b** a Right Angle Triangle has been subtracted, but it is the wrong size and rotation.

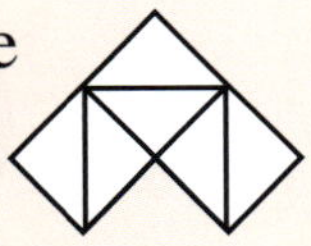

b

In **c** only one Line has been subtracted.

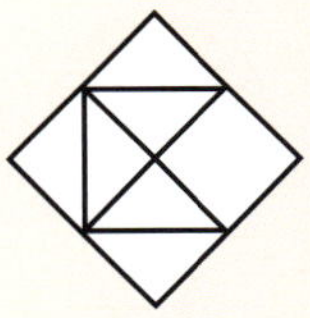

c

Step 2 - **a** and **d** need to be examined more closely.

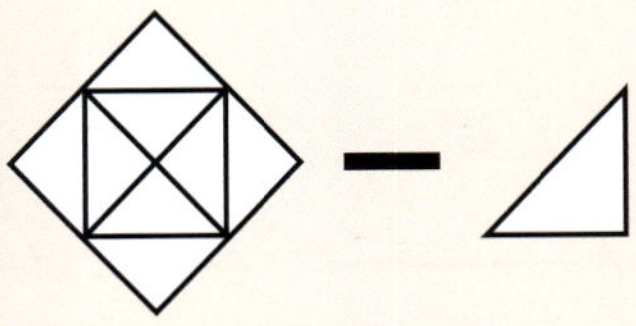

Test Figures

In **a** only two sides of the Triangle have been subtracted. This means that **a** is incorrect.

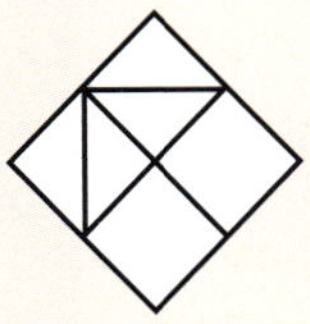

a

Step 3 - Now check **d** with the Test Figures to ensure it is the correct answer.

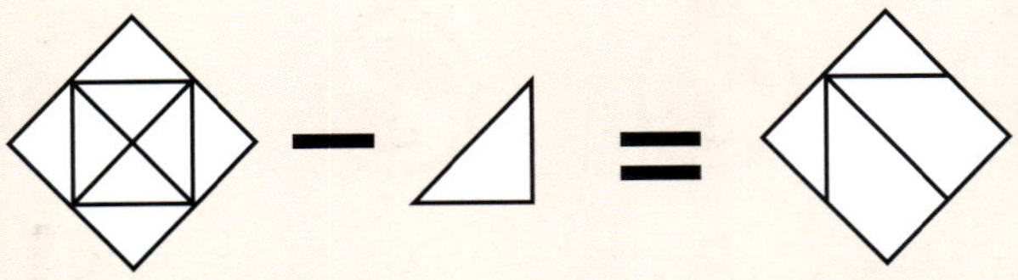

Test Figures d

After the second Test Figure has been subtracted **d** is the answer.

Exercise 23: 12

Which figure remains after the second Test Figure has been subtracted from the first Test Figure?

1)

Test Figures a b c d

Answer ____

2)

Test Figures a b c d

Answer ____

3)

Test Figures a b c d

Answer ____

4)

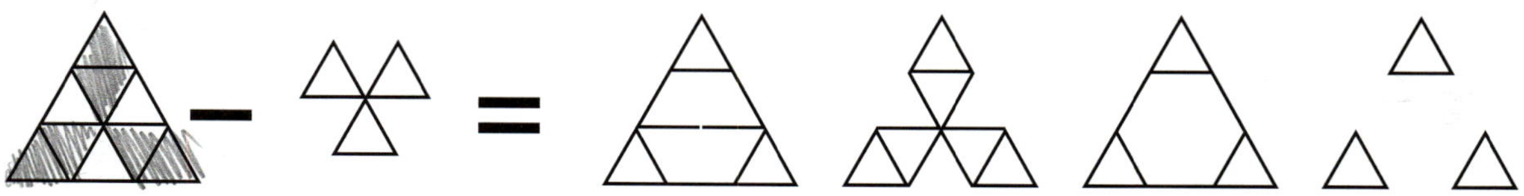

Test Figures a b c d

Answer ____

5)

Test Figures a b c d

Answer ____

6)

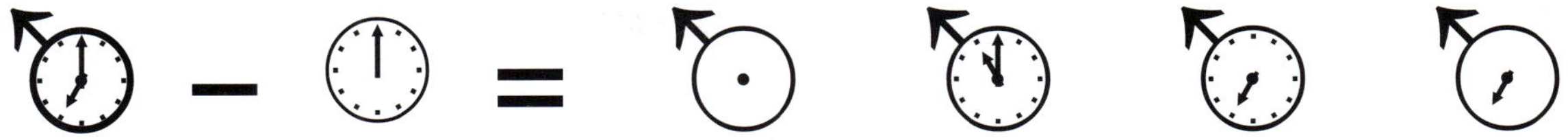

Test Figures a b c d

Answer d

7)

Test Figures a b c d

Answer c

8)

Test Figures a b c d

Answer a

9)

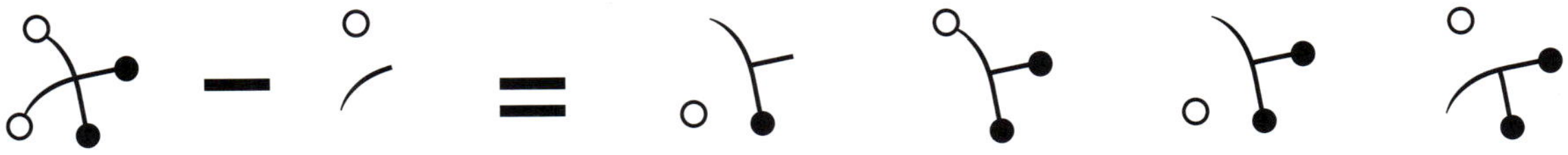

Test Figures a b c d

Answer c

10)

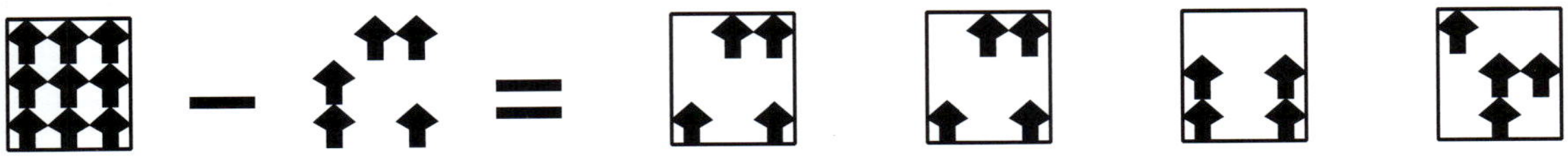

Test Figures a b c d

Answer d

Score

13. Folding a 2D Net

Folding a 2D Net questions are similar to Fitting Shapes Inside questions because they involve repositioning shapes inside another shape.

Example: Which figure on the right matches the Test Figure if the net were folded in?

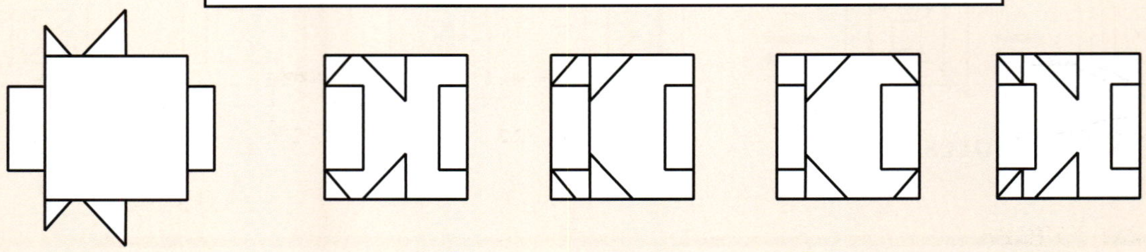

Test Figure **a** **b** **c** **d**

The best approach is to follow what the question is telling you to do. Fold in the Test Figure but do it in logical stages:

Step 1 - Fold in the shapes that are identical on both sides of the Test Figure. A quick sketch can help with this.

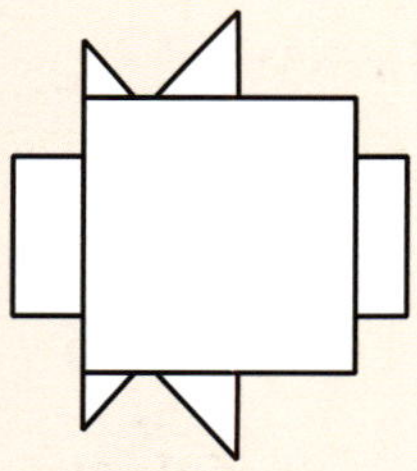

Test Figure

Fold in the Triangles at the top and bottom of the Test Figure as they are identical.

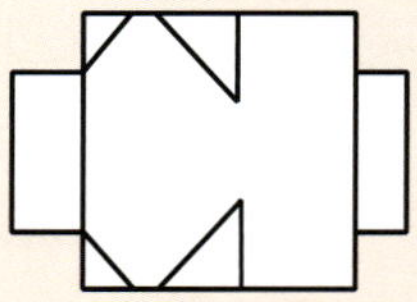

Step 2 - Now fold in the remaining parts of the Test Figure. Check the resulting figure against the options.

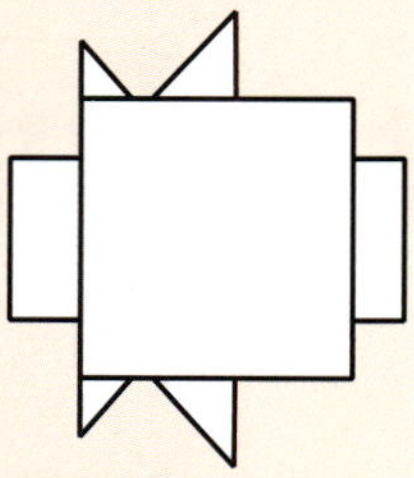

Test Figure

Fold in the two Rectangles at either end of the Test Figure.

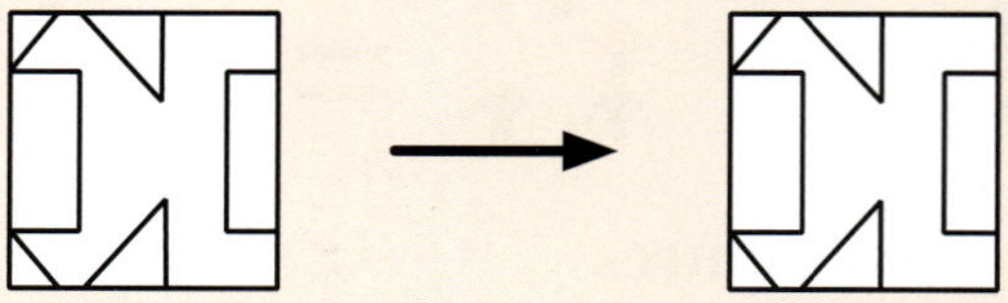

a

a matches the folded in Test Figure.

Exercise 23: 13

Which figure on the right matches the Test Figure if the net were folded in?

1)

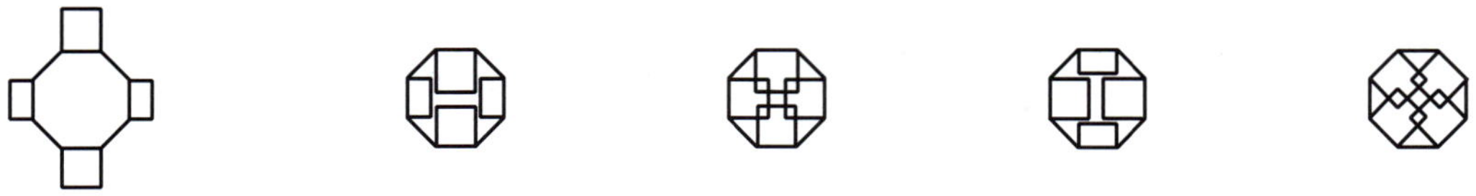

Test Figure a b c d

Answer a

2)

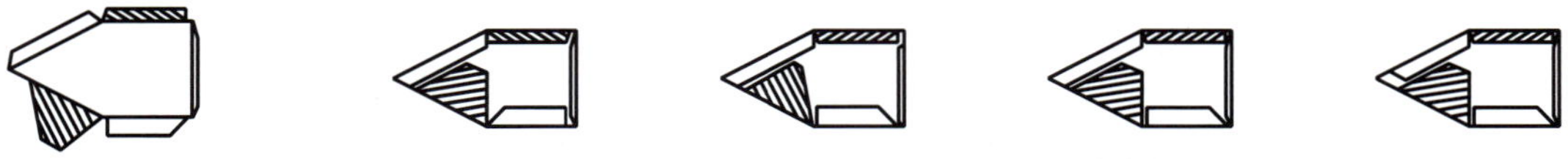

Test Figure a b c d

Answer c

3)

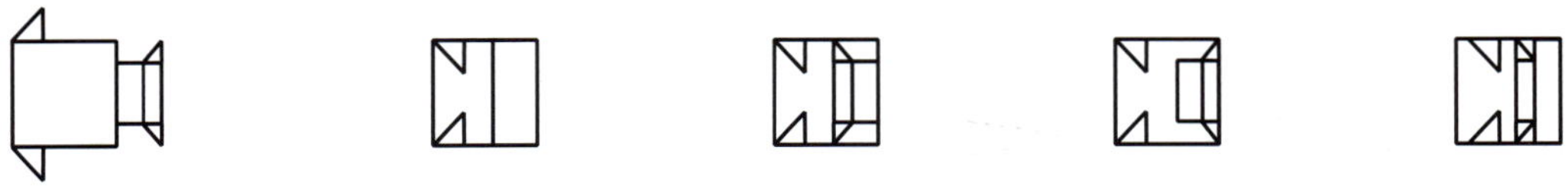

Test Figure a b c d

Answer ____

4)

Test Figure a b c d

Answer d

5)

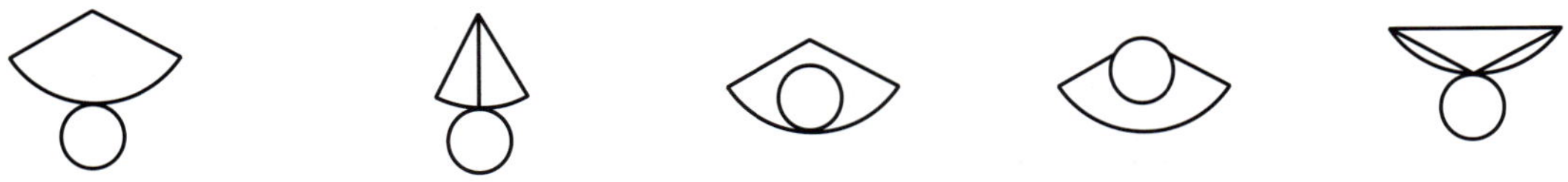

Test Figure a b c d

Answer b

6)

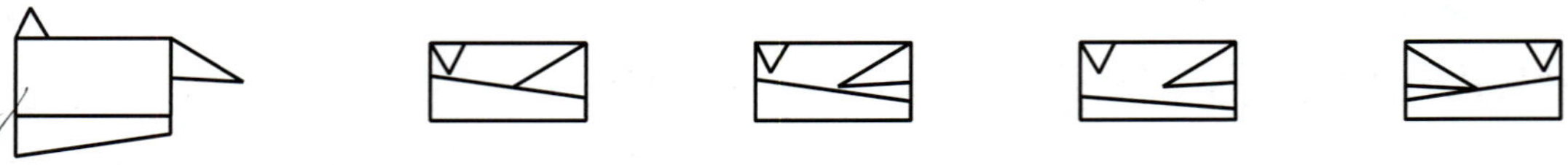

Test Figure a b c d

Answer b

7)

Test Figure a b c d

Answer b

8)

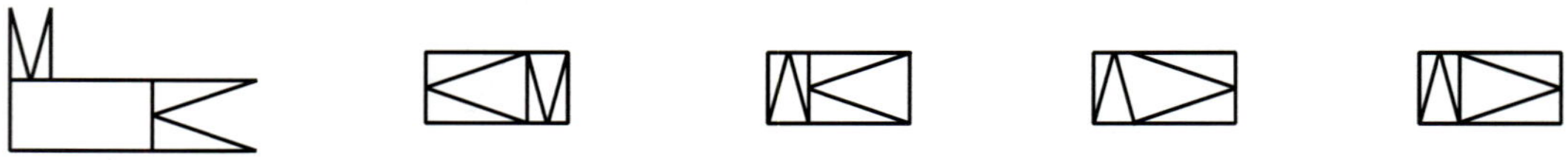

Test Figure a b c d

Answer d

9)

Test Figure a b c d

Answer a

10)

Test Figure a b c d

Answer b

Score 9

14. Unfolding a 2D Net

Unfolding a 2D Net questions are the opposite of Folding a 2D Net questions. They are solved by following the same process but in reverse.

Example: Which figure on the right matches the Test Figure if the net were unfolded?

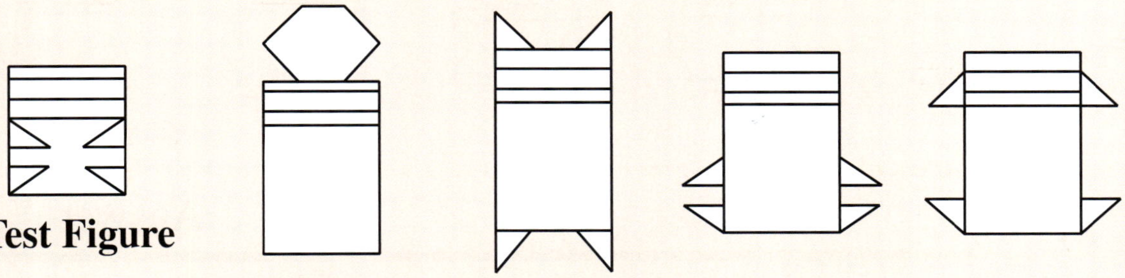

Test Figure

a b c d

The best approach is to follow what the question is telling you to do. Unfold the Test Figure but do it in logical stages:

Step 1 - Unfold the shapes that are identical on both sides of the Test Figure. Making a quick sketch can help.

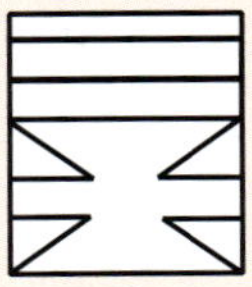

Test Figure

Unfold the Triangles on each side of the Test Figure as they are identical and this will eliminate more options.

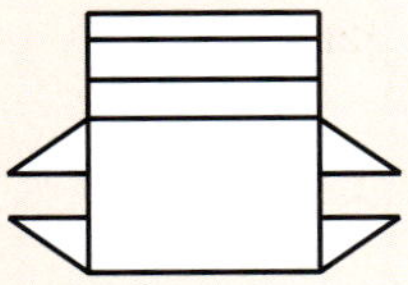

Step 2 - Now unfold the remaining part of the Test Figure. Check the resulting figure against the options.

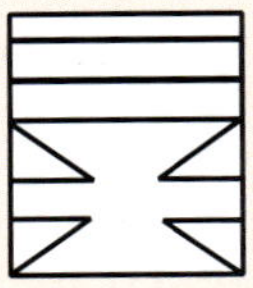

Test Figure

Unfold the Rectangles at the top of the Test Figure.

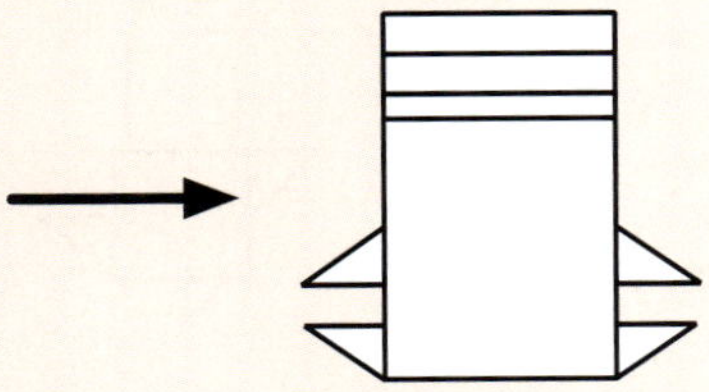

c

c matches the unfolded Test Figure.

Exercise 23: 14

Which figure on the right matches the Test Figure if the net were unfolded?

1)

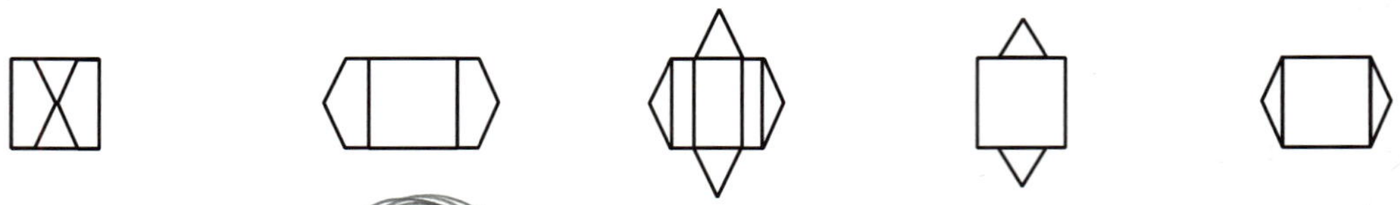

Test Figure a b c d

Answer ____

2)

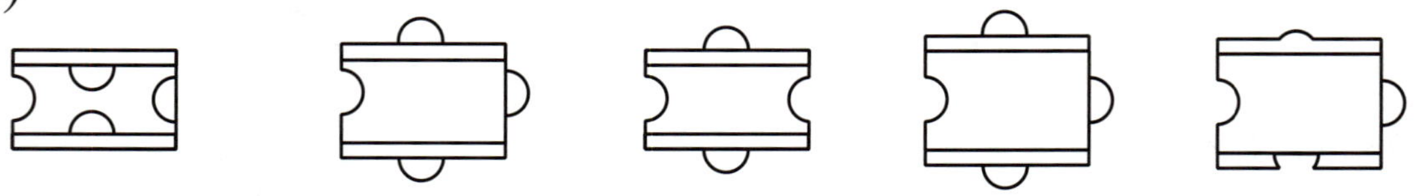

Test Figure a b c d

Answer ____

3)

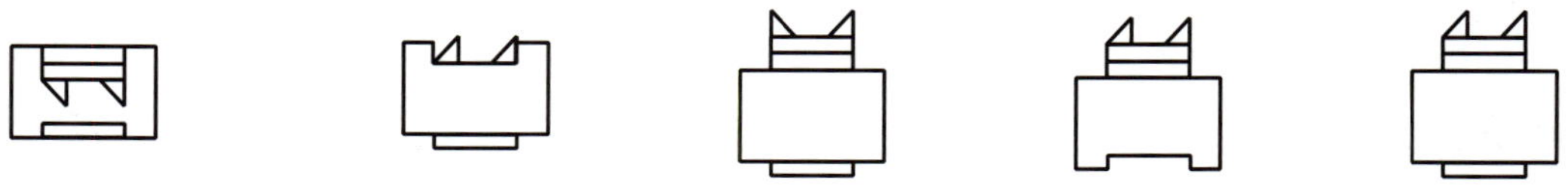

Test Figure a b c d

Answer ____

4)

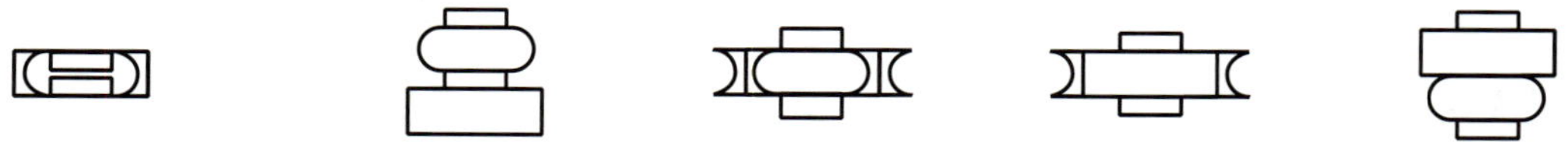

Test Figure a b c d

Answer ____

5)

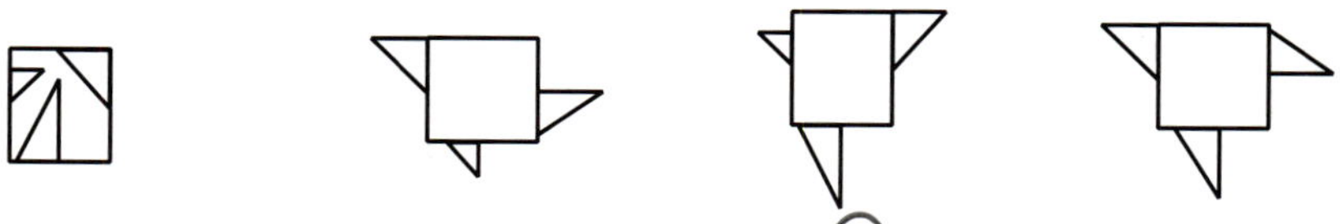

Test Figure a b c d

Answer ____

6)

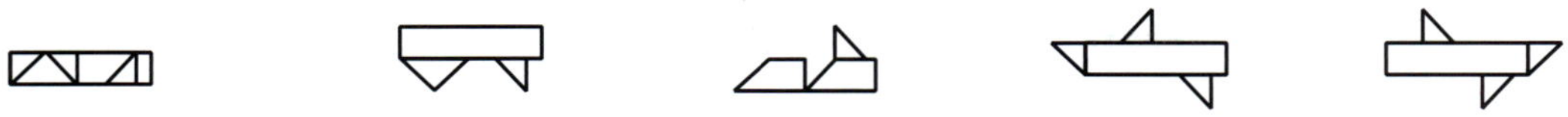

Test Figure a b c d

Answer ____

7)

Test Figure a b c d

Answer ____

8)

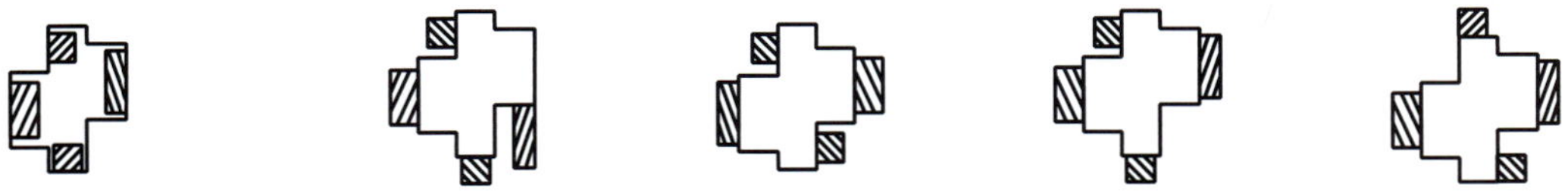

Test Figure a b c d

Answer ____

9)

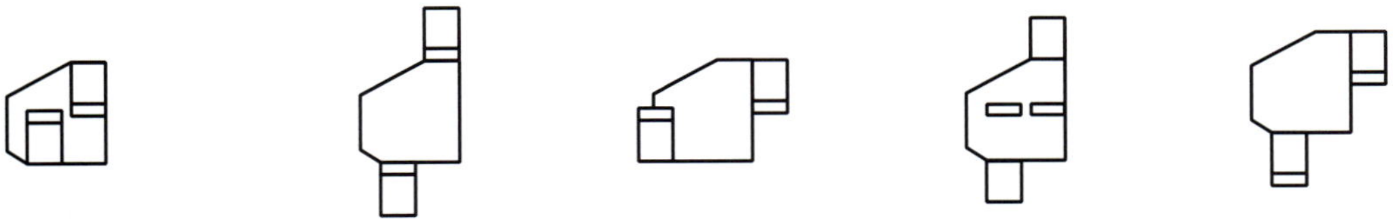

Test Figure a b c d

Answer ____

10)

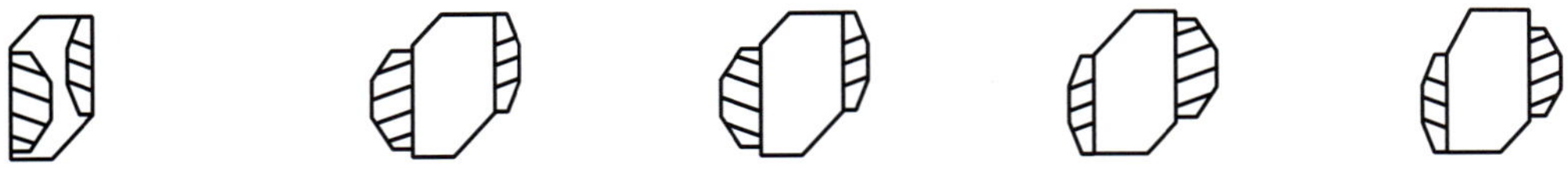

Test Figure a b c d

Answer ____

Score

Chapter Twenty-four
ROTATION & REFLECTION

Rotation and Reflection is referred to in Workbook 1 as movements that can be applied to a figure or shape. The same terms are used in geometry to define them. Rotation and Reflection includes the following question types:

Rotating a Figure • Rotating a Pattern by Degrees
Rotating a Figure by Degrees • Reflection • Symmetry

1. Rotating a Figure

Example: Which figure is a rotation of the Test Figure?

Test Figure **a** **b** **c** **d**

Step 1 - Study the Test Figure closely to see how the parts of the figure relate to each other.

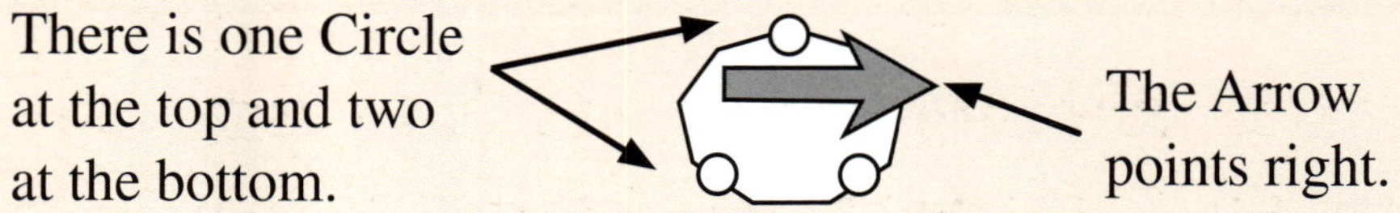

Test Figure

Step 2 - Look for alternatives that are obviously wrong by imagining where the Arrow is pointing after the Test Figure has been rotated. In both **a** and **d** the Arrow is pointing in the wrong direction.

Test Figure

The Arrow points left in **a** and **d**.

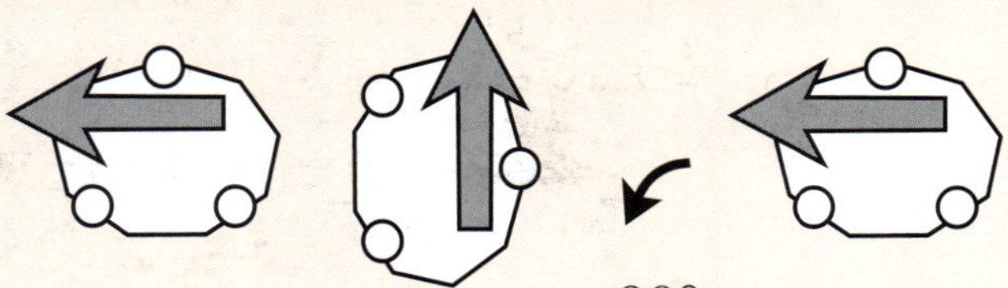

a **d** 90°

Step 3 - Now study the remaining two alternatives which are not so easy to spot.

Test Figure

Once **b** has been rotated the Arrow also points the wrong way.

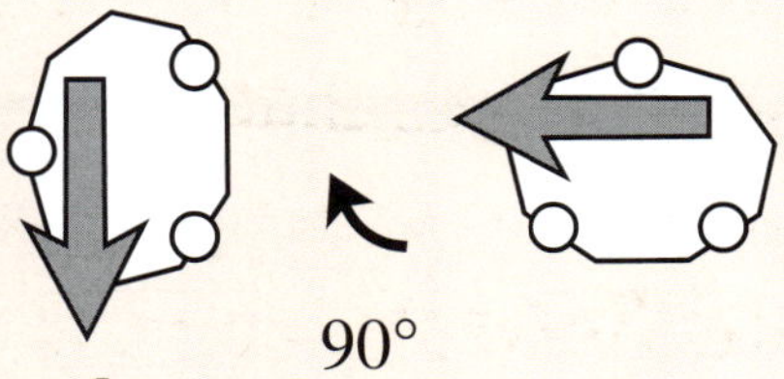

90° **b**

Step 4 - **c** appears to be the correct answer but it needs to be checked.

Test Figure

If **c** is rotated by 180° it matches the Test Figure exactly.

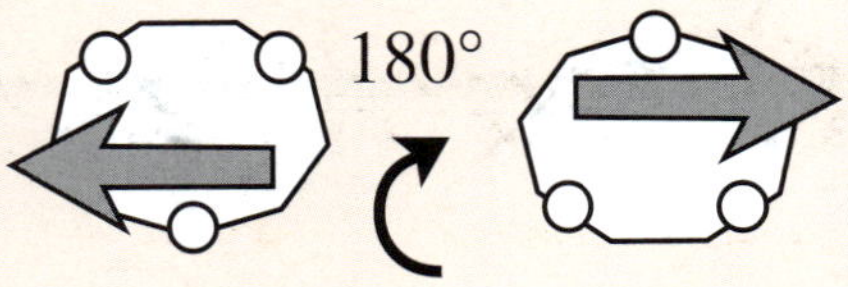

180° **c**

c is the correct rotation.

This question can be asked in a different way.

Example: Which figure is not a rotation of the Test Figure?

Test Figure

a **b** **c** **d**

a, **c** and **d** are all rotations of the Test Figure. If **b** is rotated it will not match the Test Figure.

Test Figure

Even before **b** is rotated the Arrow is in the wrong position.

180° **b**

b is not a rotation of the Test Figure.

Exercise 24: 1a

Which figure is a rotation of the Test Figure?

1)

Test Figure a b c d

Answer c

2)

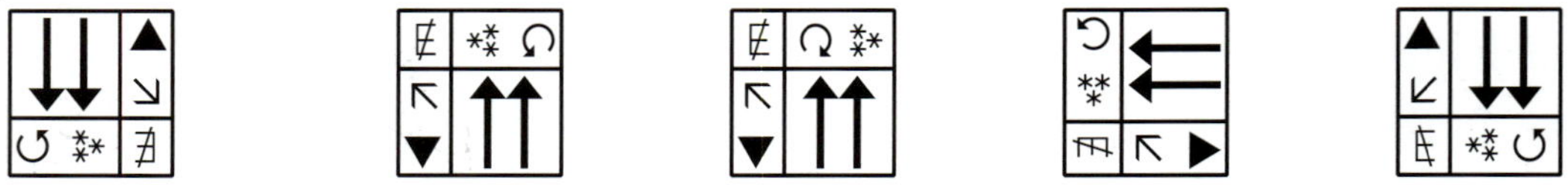

Test Figure a b c d

Answer a

3)

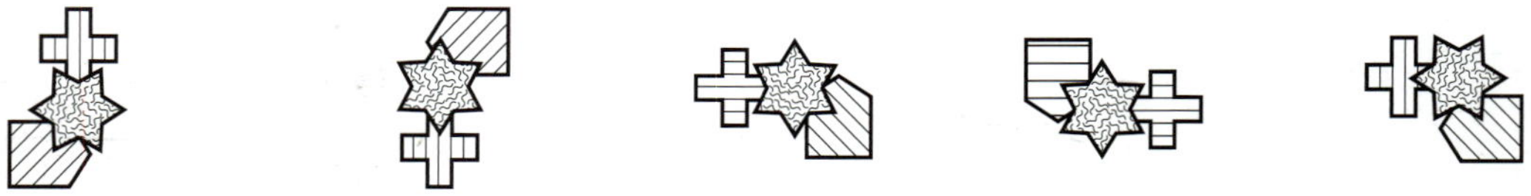

Test Figure a b c d

Answer d

4)

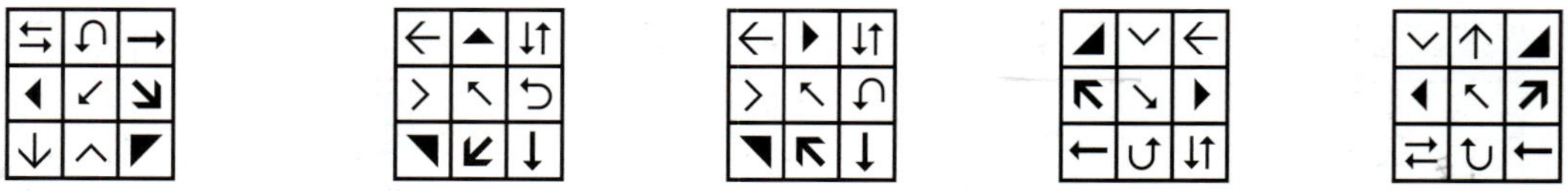

Test Figure a b c d

Answer a

5)

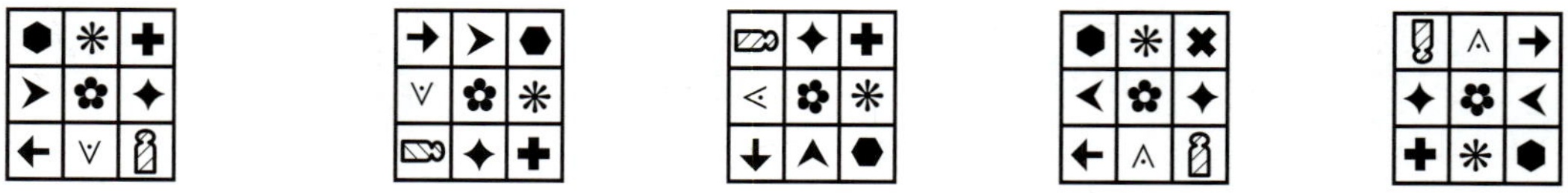

Test Figure a b c d

Answer d

Exercise 24: 1b

Which figure is not a rotation of the Test Figure?

6)

Test Figure a b c d

Answer ____

7)

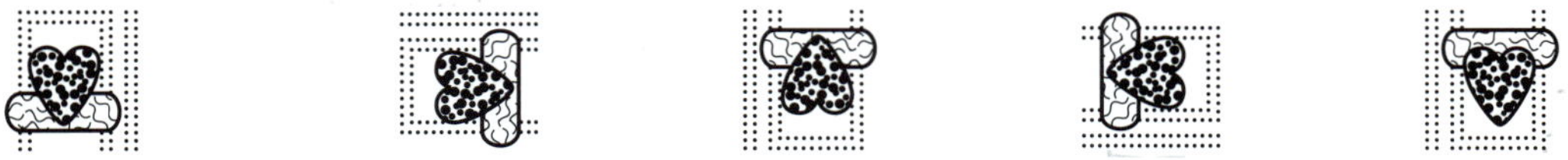

Test Figure a b c d

Answer ____

8)

Test Figure a b c d

Answer ____

9)

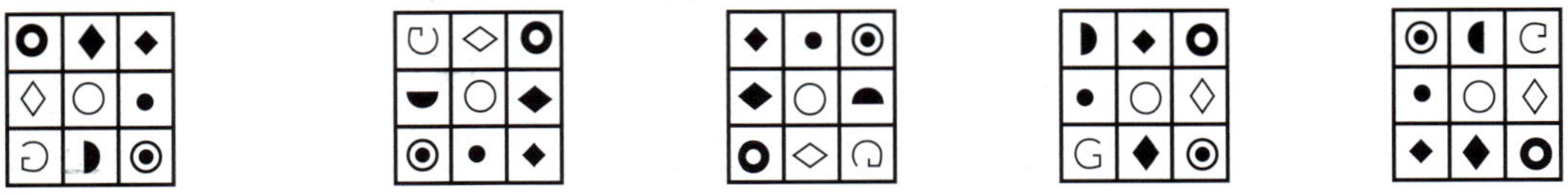

Test Figure a b c d

Answer ____

10)

Test Figure a b c d

Answer ____ Score

2. Rotating a Pattern by Degrees

Rotating a Pattern by Degrees is an extension of Hidden Pattern questions. It is more difficult because the pattern has been rotated by 90° either in a Clockwise or an Anticlockwise direction.

Example: Rotate the Test Figure as specified and draw it on the grid in the only position it will fit.

Test Figure **Grid**

In this type of rotation question the figure can only be rotated 90° Clockwise or 90° Anticlockwise.

Step 1 - Link the crosses on the Test Figure. These lines can then be rotated and redrawn on the grid. Two out of three positions are incorrect.

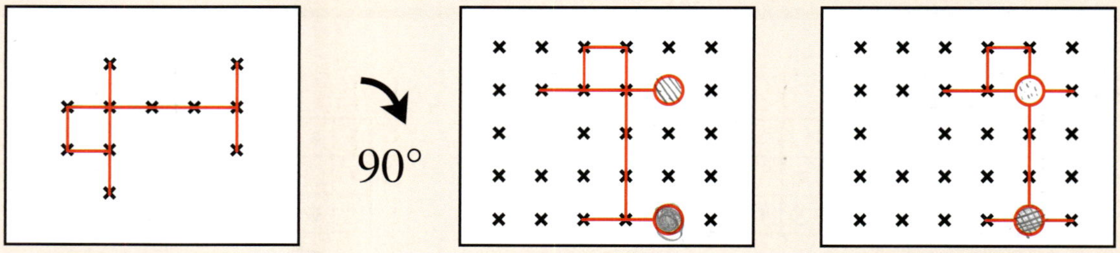

Test Figure **Position One** **Position Two**

Rotate 90° Clockwise

Circles show where the Test Figure does not fit.

Step 2 - Draw lines to test the final position on the grid.

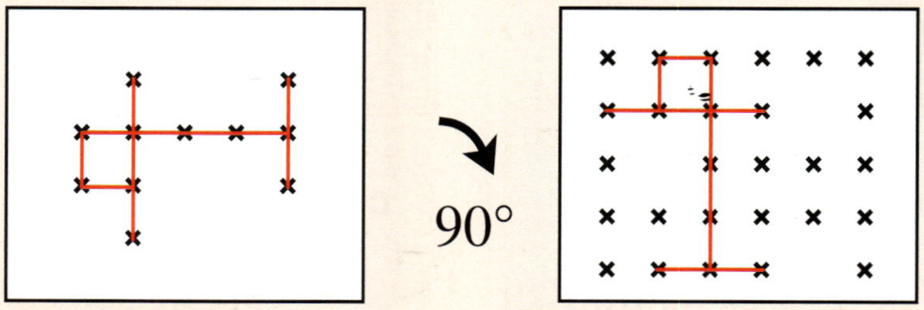

Test Figure **Position Three**

Position Three on the grid is where the Test Figure must be placed.

Exercise 24: 2

Rotate the Test Figure. Draw it on the grid in the only position it will fit.

1)

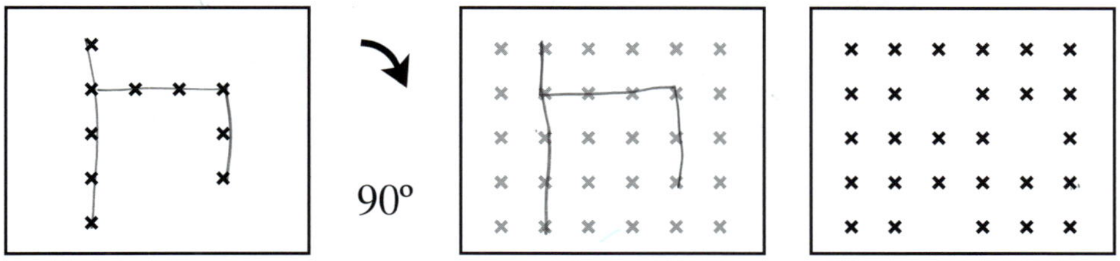

Test Figure | Working Out | Answer

2)

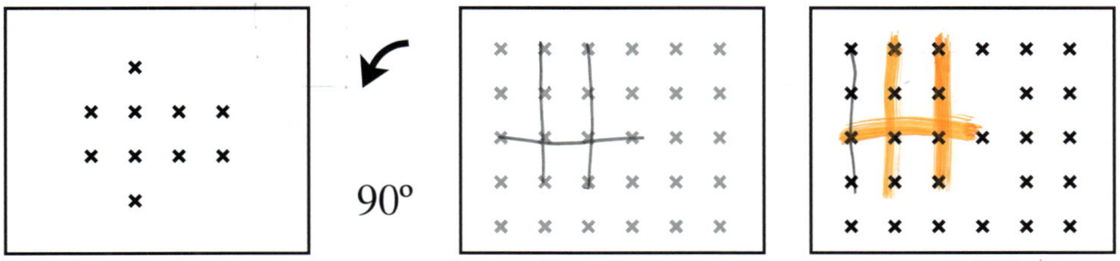

Test Figure | Working Out | ~~Answer~~

answer

3)

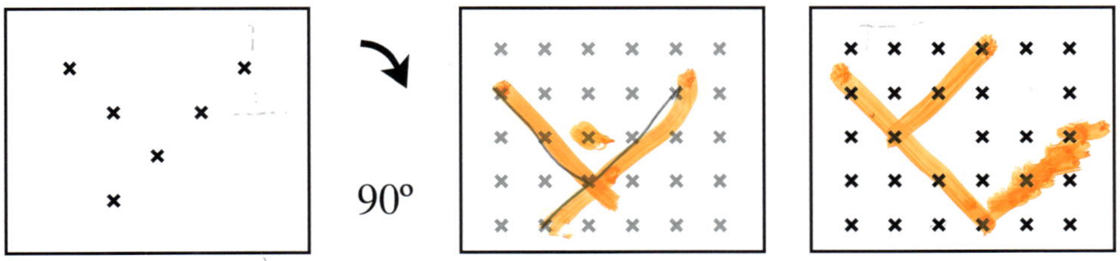

Test Figure | Working Out | Answer

4)

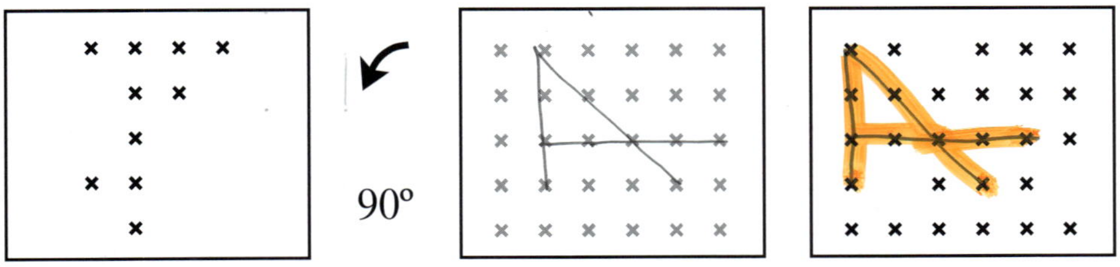

Test Figure | Working Out | Answer

5)

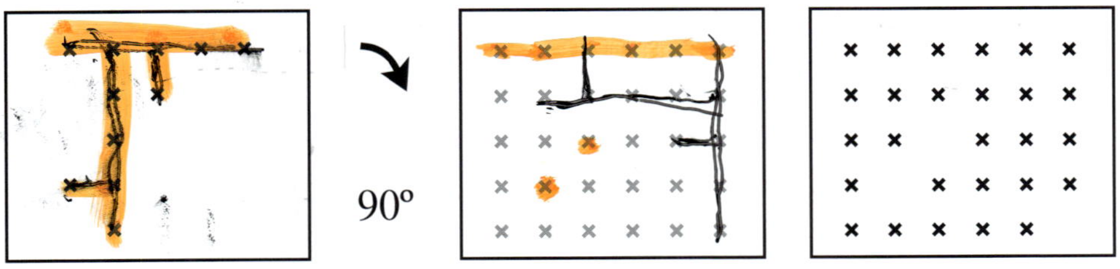

Test Figure | Working Out | Answer

6)

Test Figure

90º

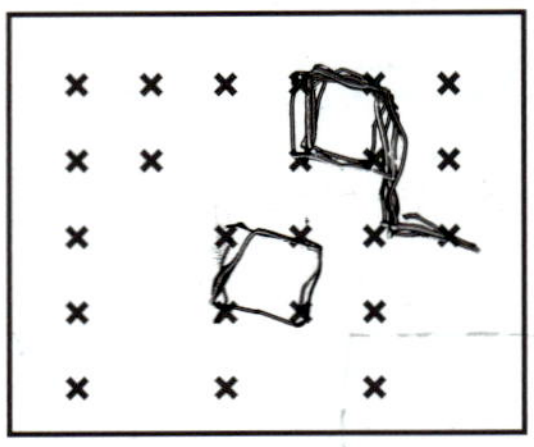

Answer

7)

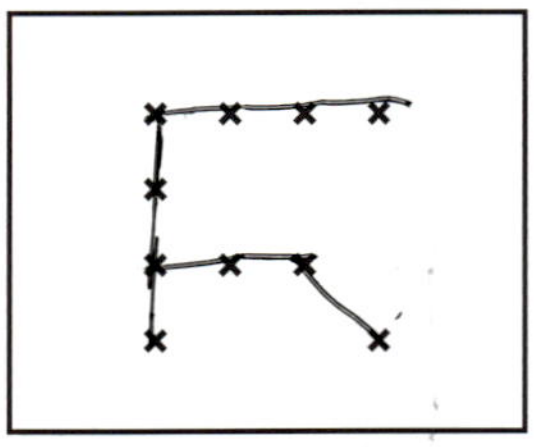

Test Figure

90º

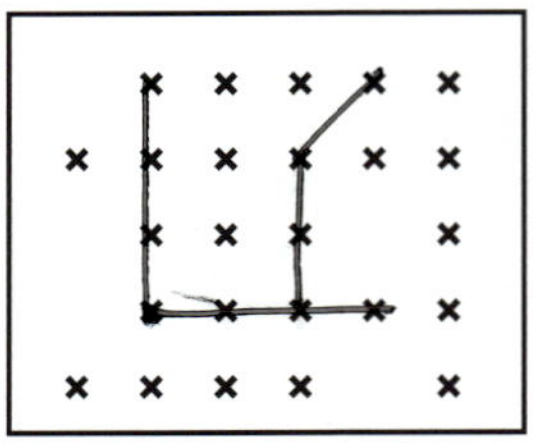

Answer

8)

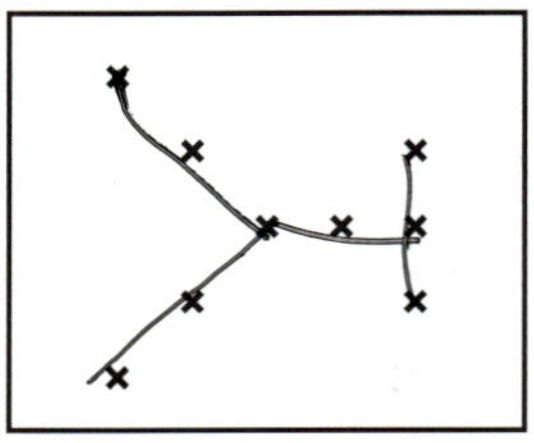

Test Figure

90º

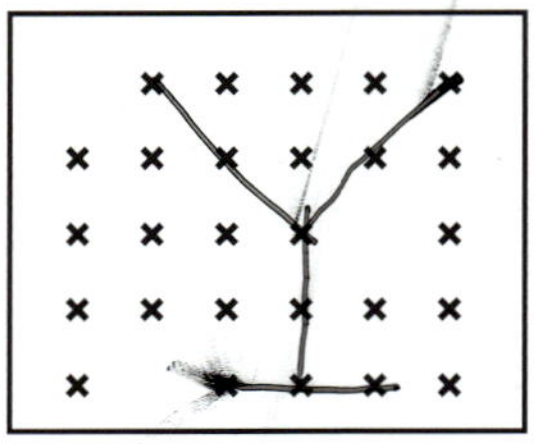

Answer

9)

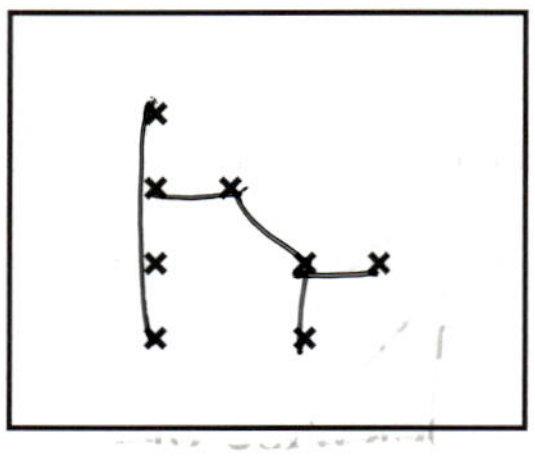

Test Figure

90º

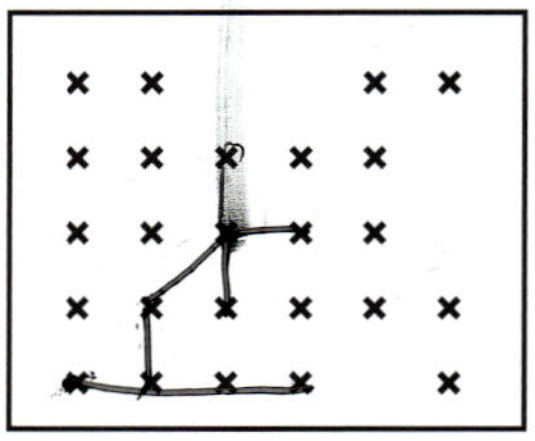

Answer

10)

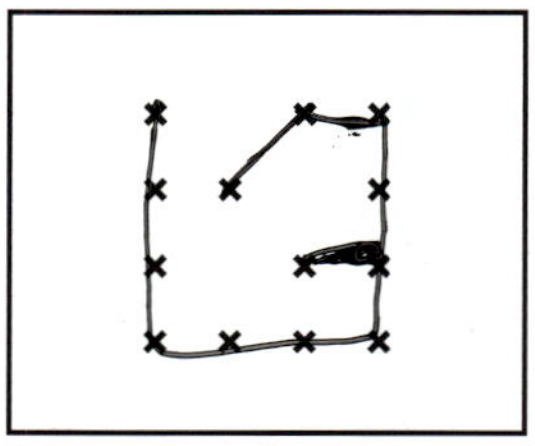

Test Figure

90º

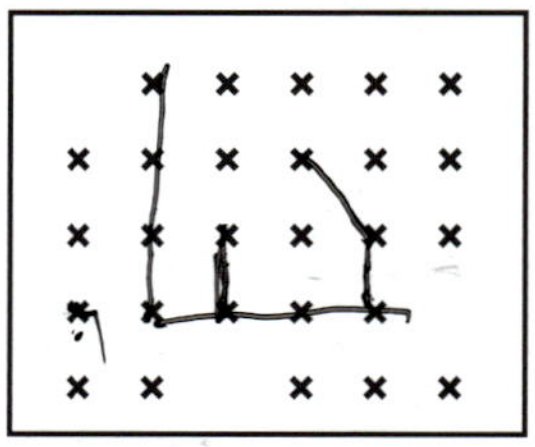

Answer

Score

3. Rotating a Figure by Degrees

Rotating a Figure by Degrees questions are an extension of Rotating a Figure questions; it involves identifying a specific rotation by degrees. Rotations are 90°, 180° and 270° Clockwise and Anticlockwise.

Example: Identify the figure that has been rotated by the specified number of degrees.

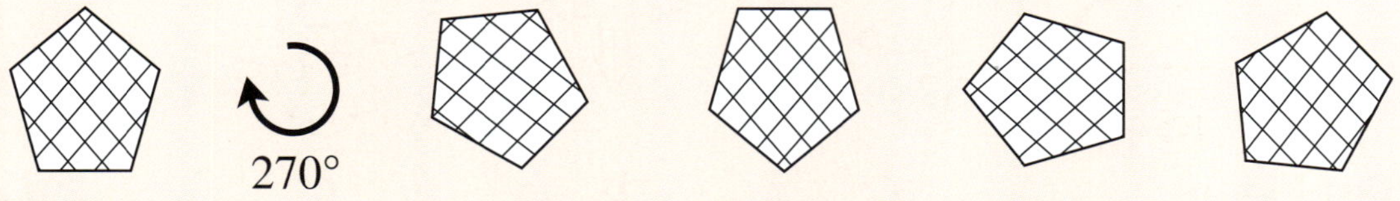

Test Figure **a** **b** **c** **d**

270° ↻ means this figure has to undergo a three-quarter Clockwise rotation or three 90° Clockwise rotations (270° in total). This can also be understood as a 90° Anticlockwise rotation.

Step 1 - Look for alternatives that can be easily eliminated. **a** and **b** are obviously incorrect.

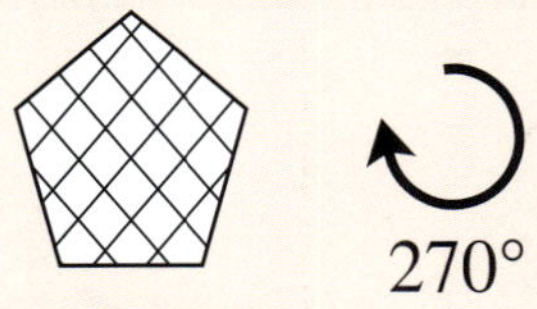

Test Figure

a has been rotated Anticlockwise by 45°.

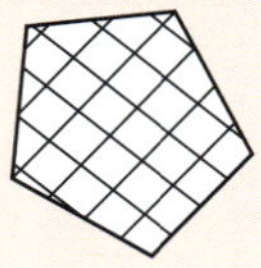

a

b has been rotated 180° (this can be either Clockwise or Anticlockwise).

b

Step 2 - Now focus on the last two alternatives. **c** and **d** have closer rotations in degrees.

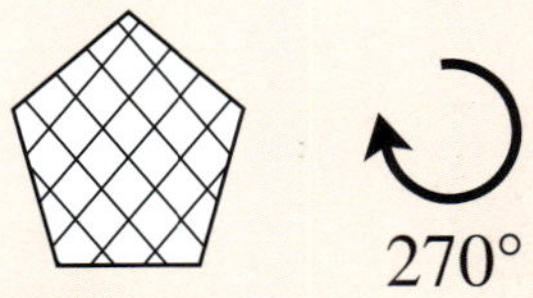

Test Figure

d has been rotated either Anticlockwise by 135° or Clockwise by 225°.

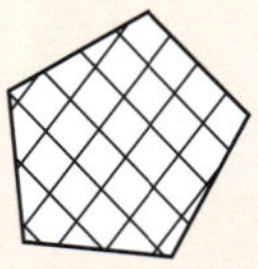

d

c has been rotated either Anticlockwise by 90° or Clockwise by 270°.

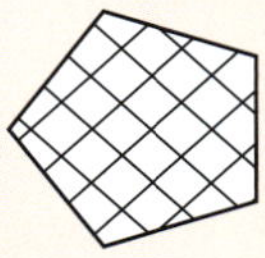

c

c is the correct rotation of the Test Figure because it has been rotated 270° Clockwise.

Exercise 24: 3

Identify the figure that is the correct rotation of the Test Figure.

1)

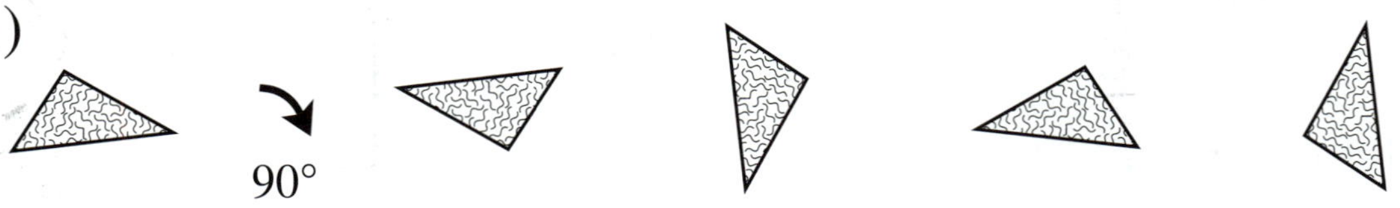

Test Figure a b c d

Answer b

2)

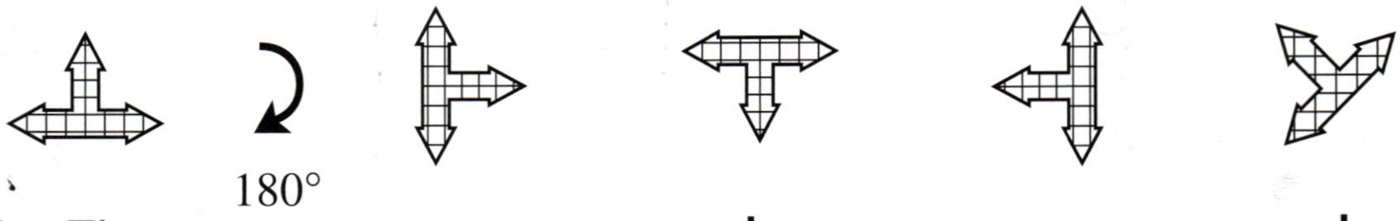

Test Figure a b c d

Answer b

3)

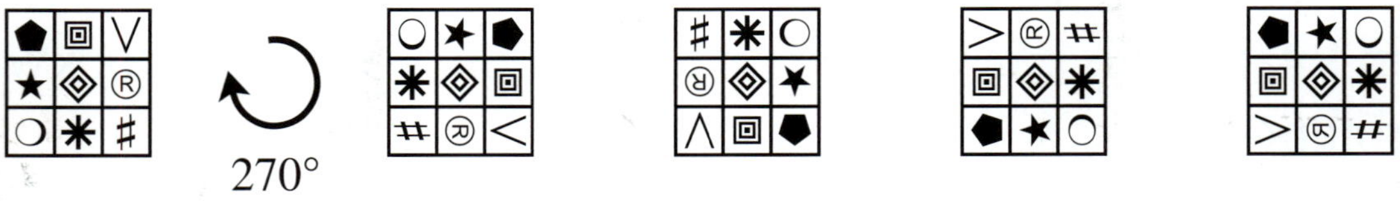

Test Figure a b c d

Answer a

4)

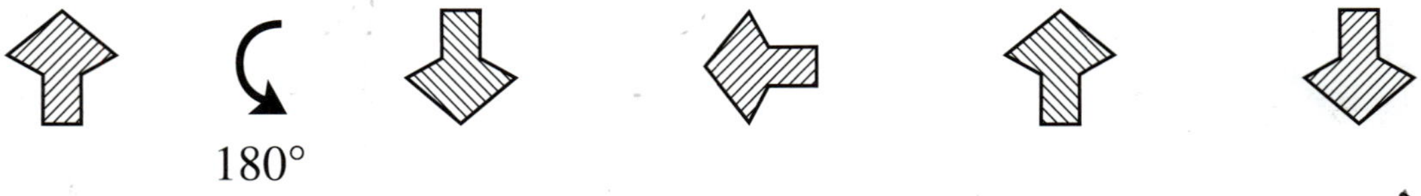

Test Figure a b c d

Answer d

5)

Test Figure a b c d

Answer a

6)

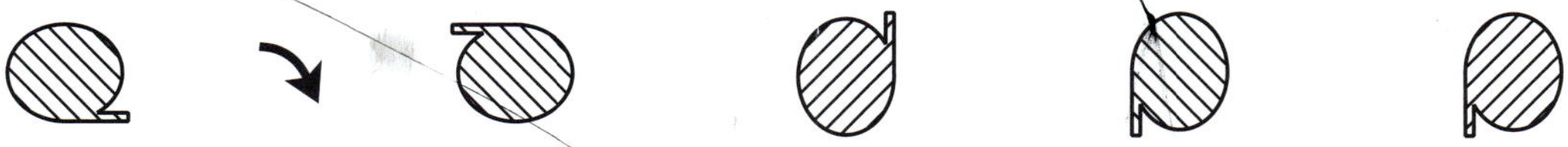

90°

Test Figure **a** **b** **c** **d**

Answer d

7)

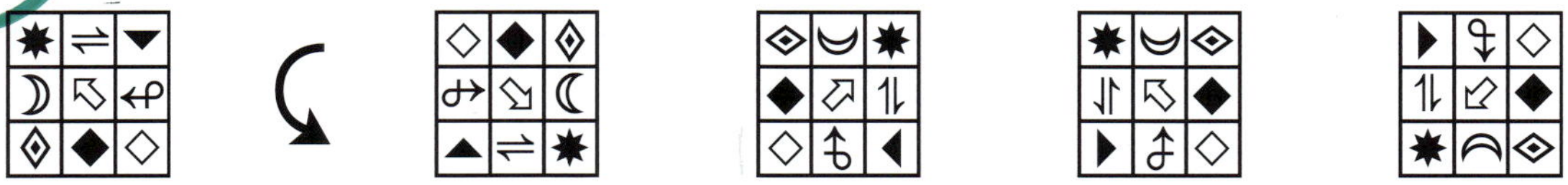

180°

Test Figure **a** **b** **c** **d**

Answer a

8)

270°

Test Figure **a** **b** **c** **d**

Answer c

9)

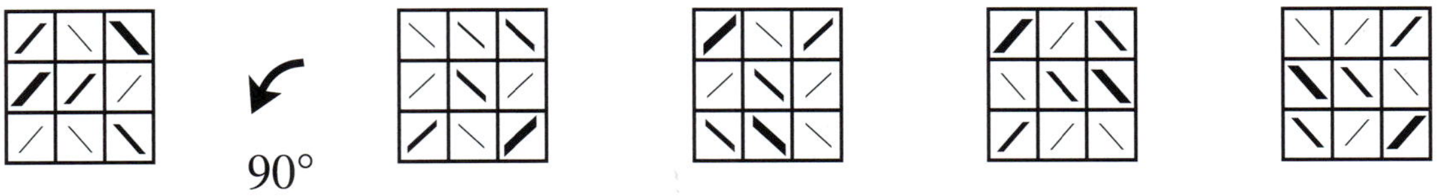

90°

Test Figure **a** **b** **c** **d**

Answer b

10)

270°

Test Figure **a** **b** **c** **d**

Answer d

Score

4. Reflection

Reflection is one of the five movements that can be applied to shapes or figures; these are explained in Workbook 1. However, it can also occur as a specific question type as featured below. It is recognised as a geometrical movement within mathematics.

Example: Which figure is a reflection of the Test Figure?

Test Figure **a** **b** **c** **d**

Reflection can be understood as a mirror image of a figure. The line separating the Test Figure from the options is a Line of Reflection or Axis of Symmetry.

Step 1 - Look for alternatives that can be easily eliminated.
a and **b** are obviously incorrect.

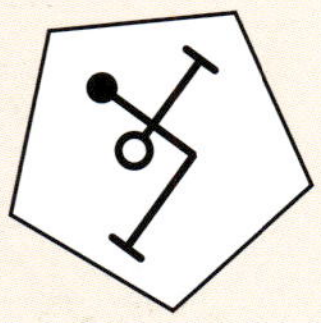

Test Figure

The Pentagons and the enclosed shapes in both **a** and **b** do not reflect.

a

b

Step 2 - Now focus on the last two alternatives.
c and **d** need to be examined more closely.

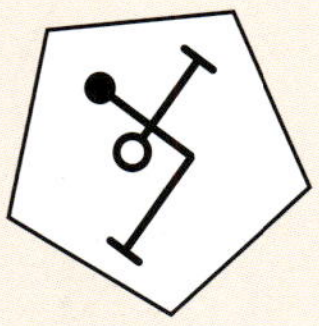

Test Figure

The Pentagon in **c** does reflect but the enclosed shapes do not.

c

Every part of **d** is a reflection of the Test Figure.

d

d is a reflection of the Test Figure.

Exercise 24: 4

Which figure is a reflection of the Test Figure?

1)

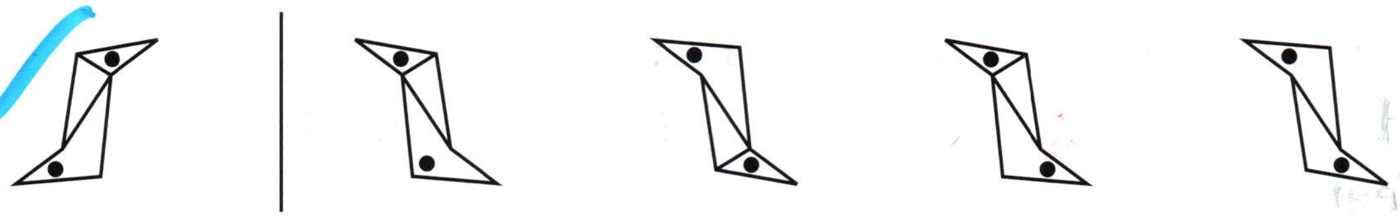

Test Figure | a | b | c | d

Answer c

2)

Test Figure | a | b | c | d

Answer b

3)

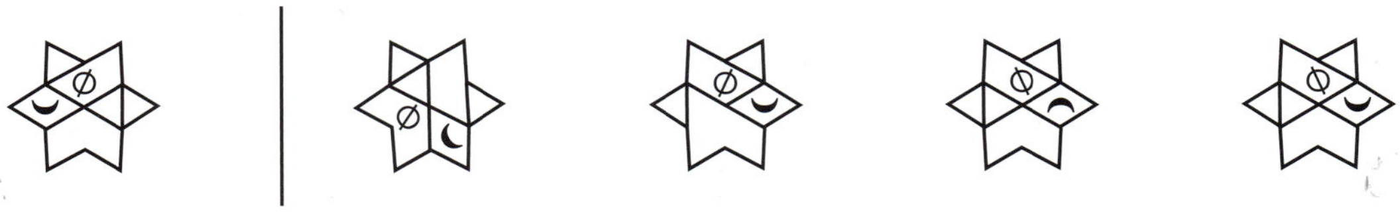

Test Figure | a | b | c | d

Answer D

4)

Test Figure | a | b | c | d

Answer a

5)

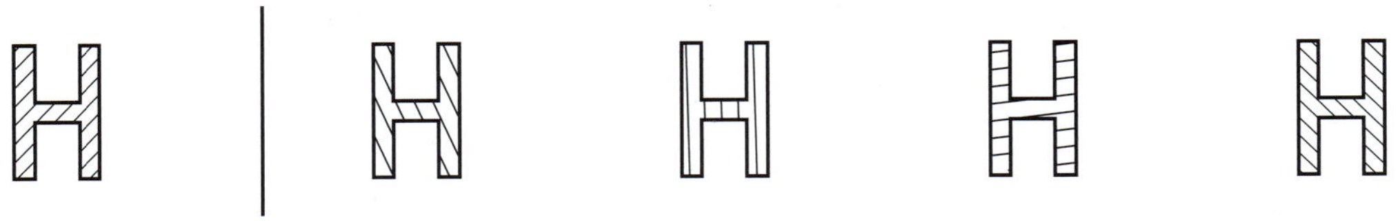

Test Figure | a | b | c | d

Answer d

6)

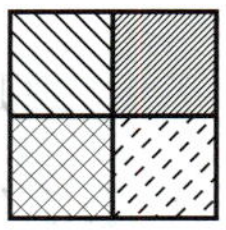

Test Figure | a | b | c | d

Answer b

7)

Test Figure | a | b | c | d

Answer d

8)

Test Figure | a | b | c | d

Answer c

9)

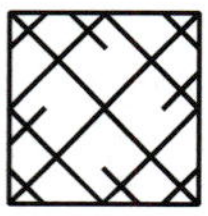

Test Figure | a | b | c | d

Answer a

10)

Test Figure | a | b | c | d

Answer a

Score

5. Symmetry

Symmetry is a variation on Reflection and is also classed as one of the five movements that can be applied to a shape or figure. This is referred to in Workbook 1. Just like reflection, symmetry can appear as a specific question type. It involves identifying whether a shape or figure is symmetrical (has a Line or Axis of Symmetry). If it has no Line(s) of Symmetry it is asymmetrical.

Example: Which shape is asymmetrical (has no line(s) of symmetry)?

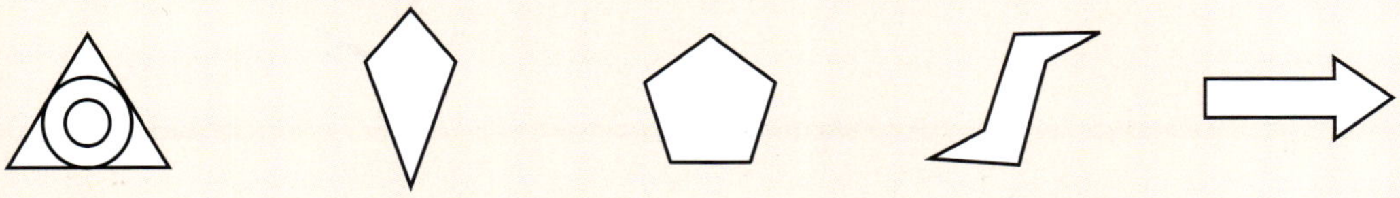

a **b** **c** **d** **e**

Step 1 - Sketch the line(s) of symmetry on the shapes. This works for **a**, **b**, **c** and **e**.

Both sides of the line(s) of symmetry are a mirror reflection of each other.

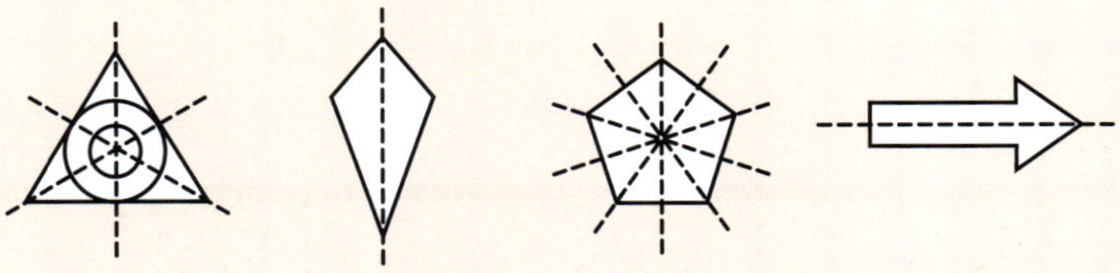

a **b** **c** **e**

Step 2 - Check the remaining shape has no line(s) of symmetry. As these cannot be drawn on **d** it is the correct answer.

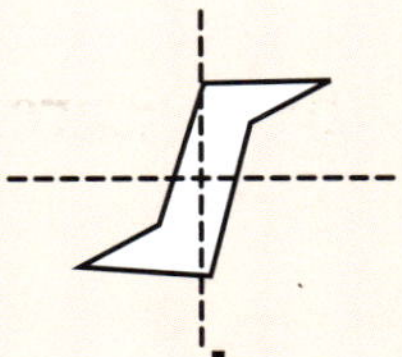

d

The question can be asked in a different way.

Example: Which shape is symmetrical (has a line of symmetry)?

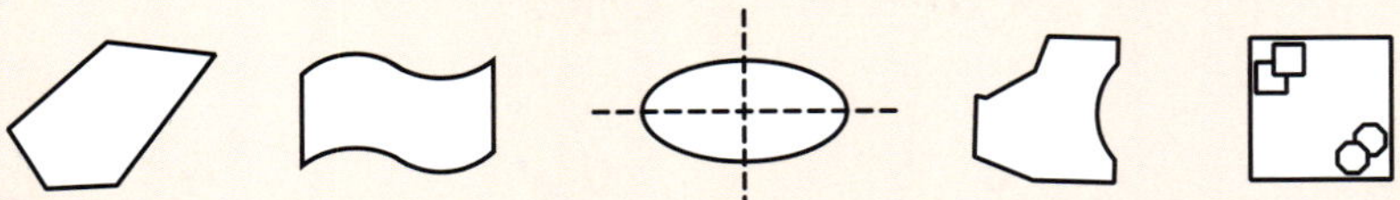

a **b** **c** **d** **e**

c is the correct answer.

Exercise 24: 5a

Which shape is asymmetrical (has no line(s) of symmetry)?

1)

a b c d e

Answer c

2)

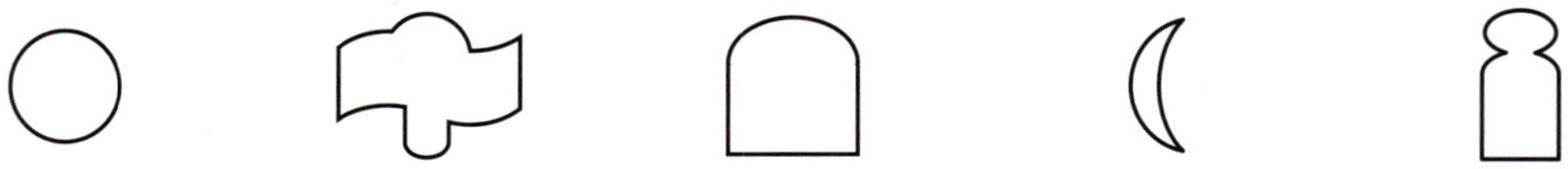

a b c d e

Answer b

3)

a b c d e

Answer c

4)

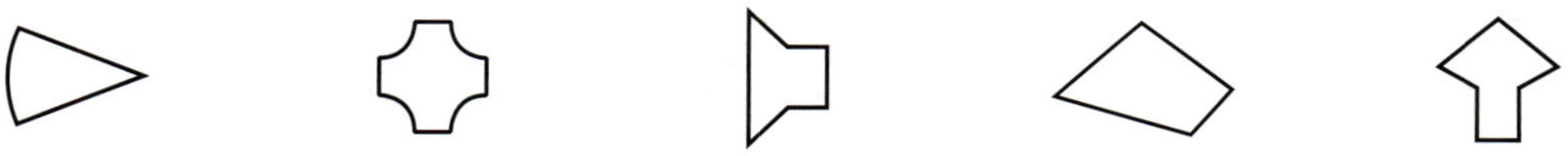

a b c d e

Answer d

5)

a b c d e

Answer a

Exercise 24: 5b

Which shape is symmetrical (has line(s) of symmetry)?

6)

a b c d e

Answer D

7)

a b c d e

Answer c

8)

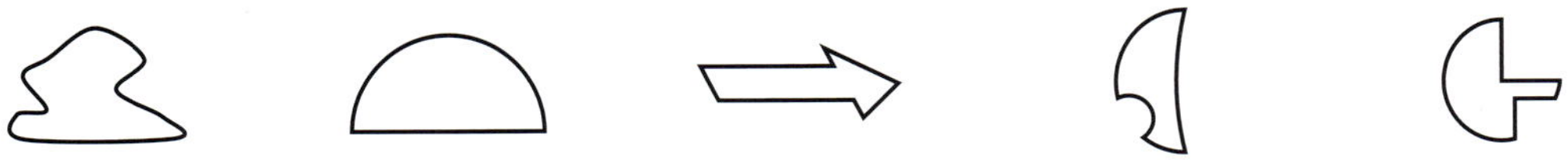

a b c d e

Answer b

9)

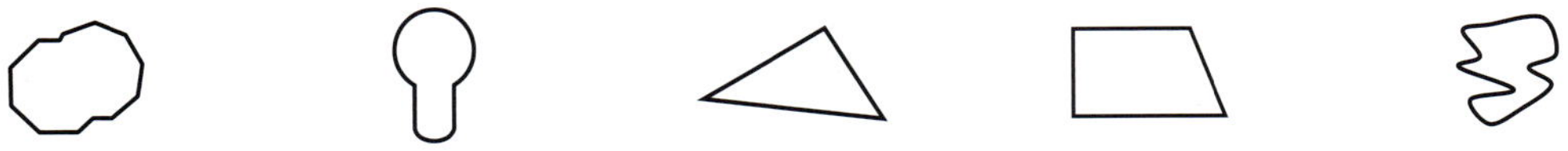

a b c d e

Answer b

10)

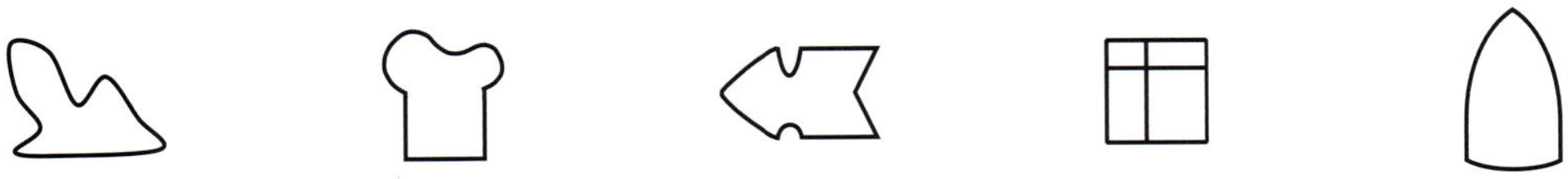

a b c d e

Answer e

Score

Chapter Twenty-five
MORE ANALOGIES

Analogy questions are fully explained in Workbook 2. However, there are two further variations of the Analogy question type:

Bug Analogy • Double Example Analogy

Bug Analogies work in exactly the same way as standard Analogies except they are created around an insect theme.

1. Bug Analogy

Example: Which figure completes the analogy?

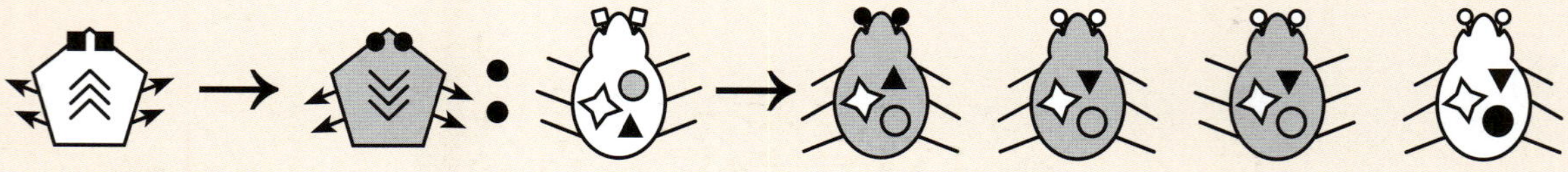

Test Figures **a** **b** **c** **d**

Step 1 - Establish the analogy rules from the Test Figures.

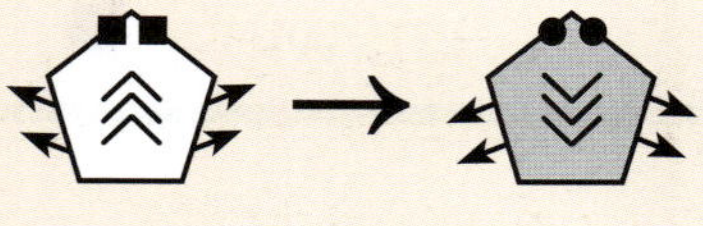

Test Figures

There are four rules in this analogy:
1. The White Fill in the Pentagon becomes Grey.
2. The three Chevrons either rotate 180° or are flipped Vertically.
3. The Square eyes become Circle eyes.
4. The Bug legs point down instead of up.

Step 2 - Apply the rules to eliminate the options.

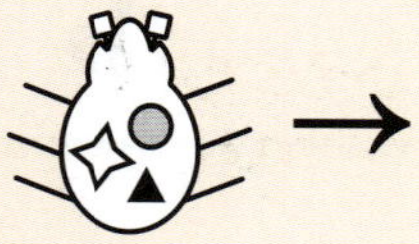

a breaks rules 2 and 3. The Triangle should either rotate 180° or be flipped Vertically and the eyes should have a White Fill.

a

c breaks rule 4. The Bug legs should point down and not up.

c

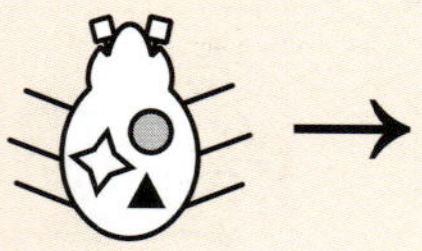

d breaks rule 1. The White Fill in the Pentagon should be Grey.

d

b follows all four rules.

b

b completes the analogy.

Exercise 25: 1 Which figure completes the analogy?

1)

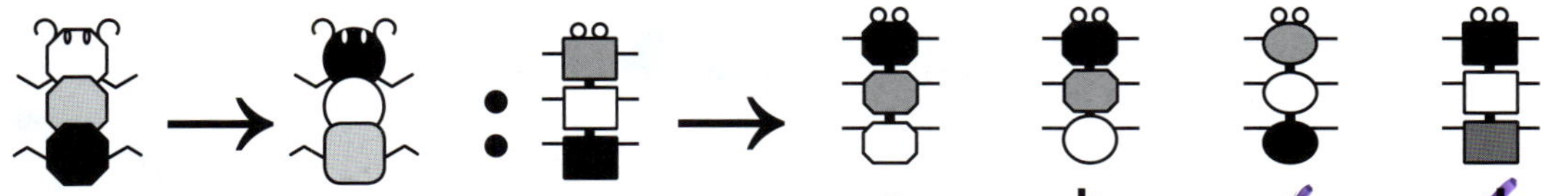

Test Figures

a b c d

Answer b

2)

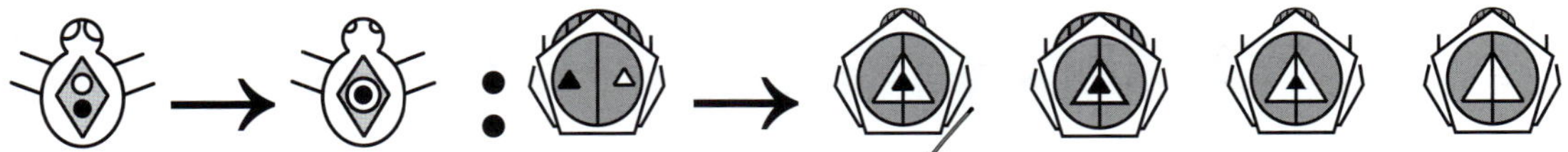

Test Figures

a b c d

Answer c

3)

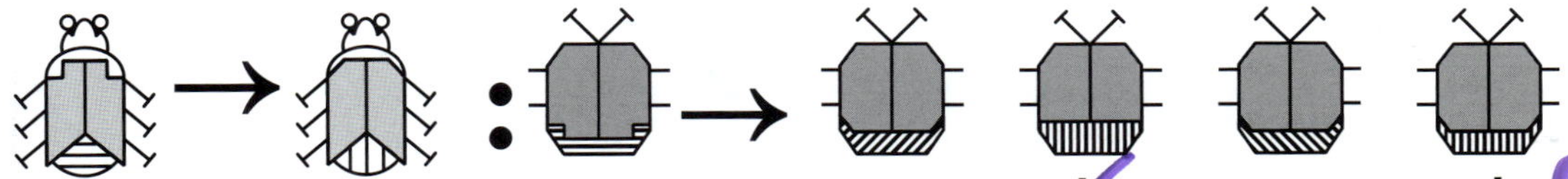

Test Figures

a b c d

Answer d

4)

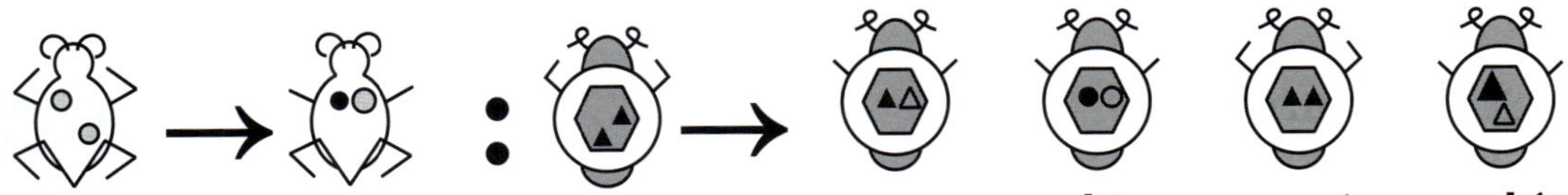

Test Figures

a b c d

Answer a

5)

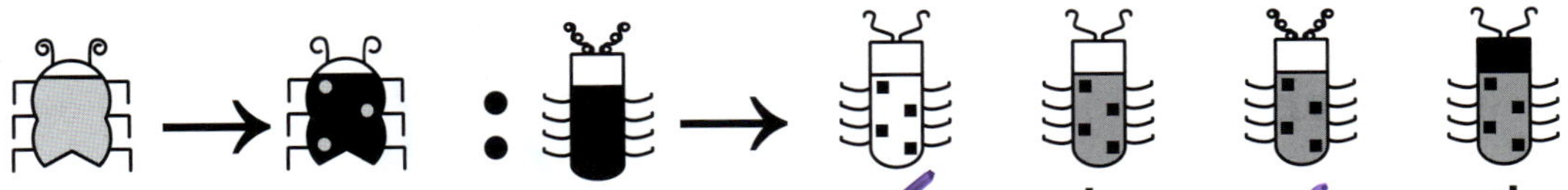

Test Figures

a b c d

Answer b

6)

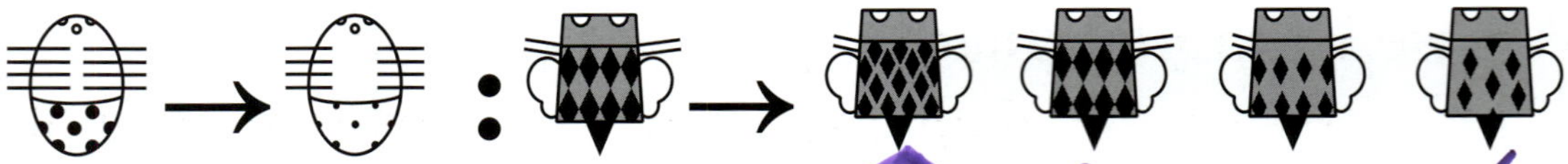

Test Figures

a b c d

Answer c

7)

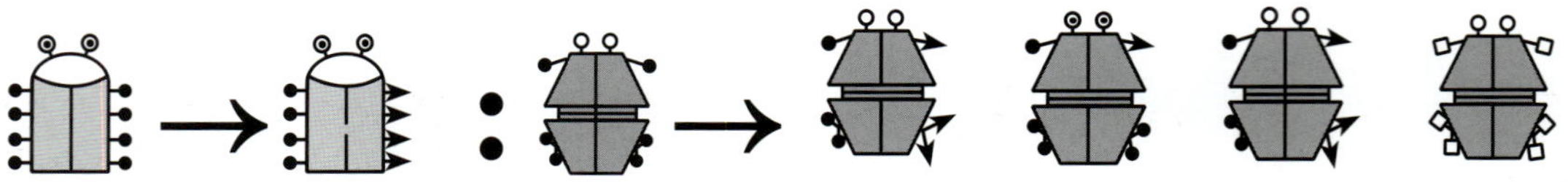

a b c d

Test Figures

Answer a

8)

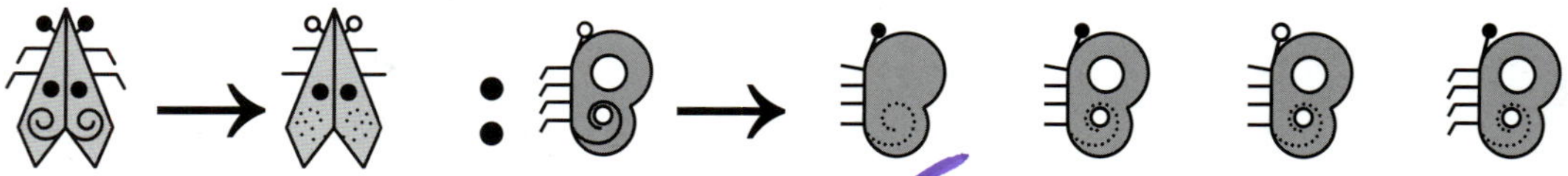

a b c d

Test Figures

Answer b

9)

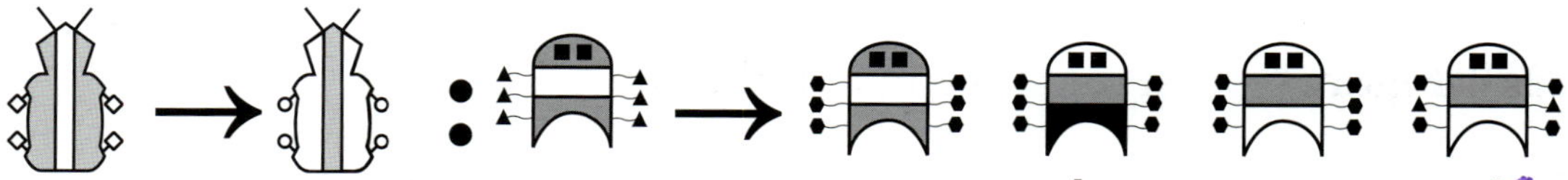

a b c d

Test Figures

Answer c

10)

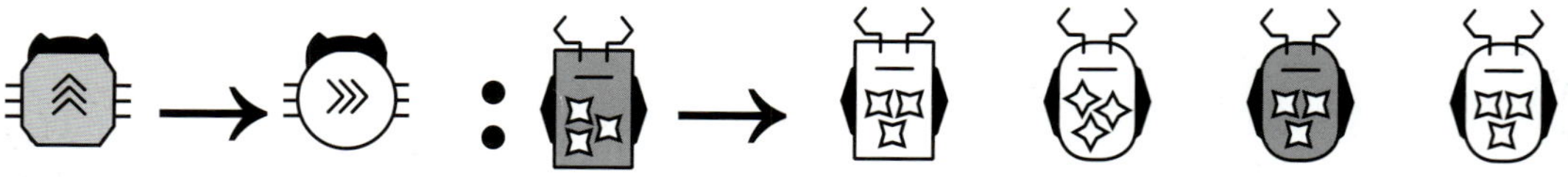

a b c d

Test Figures

Answer d

Score

2. Double Example Analogy

Double Example Analogy questions can combine elements of repetitive or cumulative series with the analogy type of question.

Example: Which figure completes the analogy?

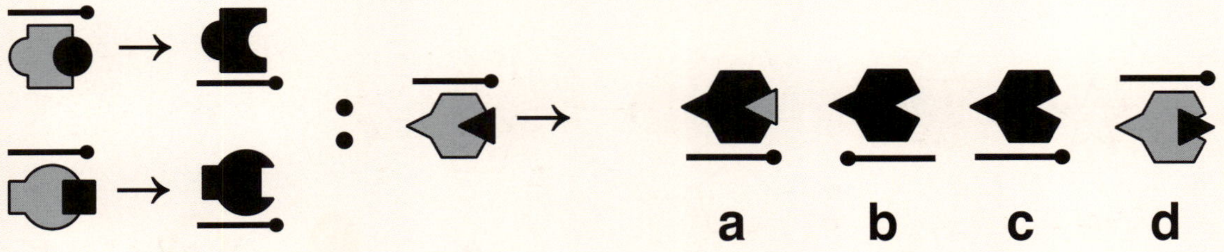

Test Figures

Step 1 - Establish the analogy rules from the first example.

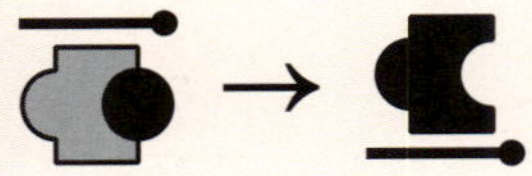

Test Figures

There are three rules in this analogy:

1. The Grey Fill in the large shape becomes Black.
2. The large shape and the Matchstick Shape swap places.
3. The Black Fill Circle is subtracted from the figure.

Step 2 - Check the rules using the second example.

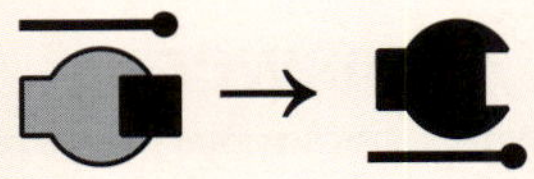

Test Figures

The rules are confirmed in the second analogy example.
Rules 1 and 2 are identical.
For rule 3 a Black Fill Square is subtracted from the figure instead of a Black Fill Circle.

Step 3 - Now apply the rules to eliminate the options.

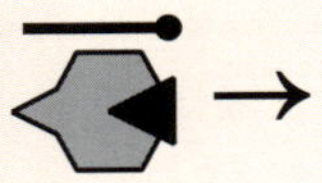

a breaks rule 3. The Triangle has not been subtracted from the figure.

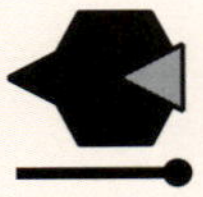

a

b breaks rule 2 as the Matchstick Shape faces the wrong way.

b

d breaks rules 1 and 3. The fill is not Black and the Triangle has not been subtracted.

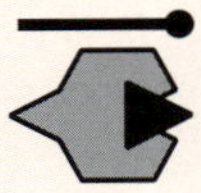

d

c follows all three rules.

c

c completes the analogy.

Exercise 25: 2 Which figure completes the analogy?

1)

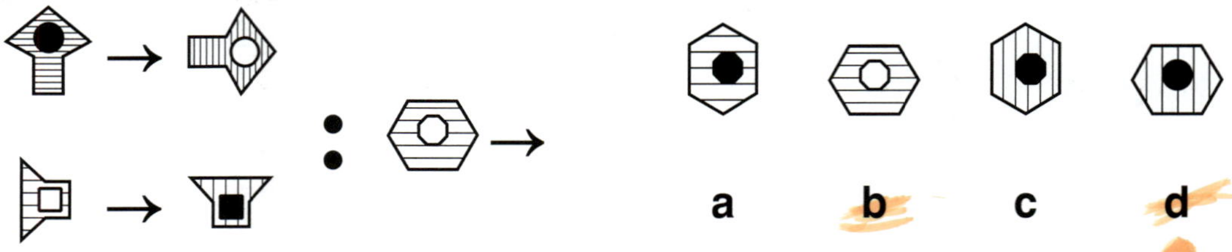

Test Figures

Answer ____

2)

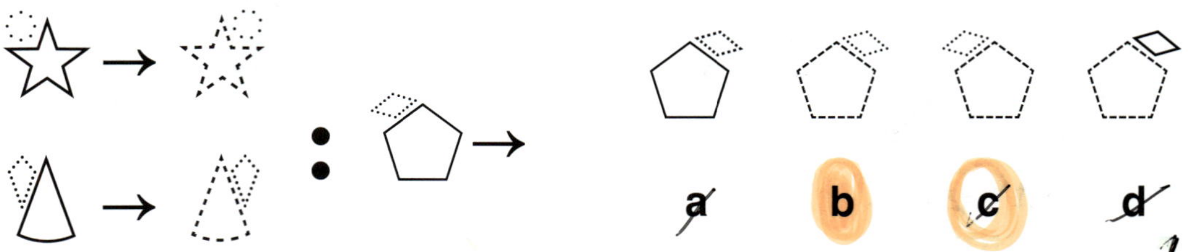

Test Figures

Answer ____

3)

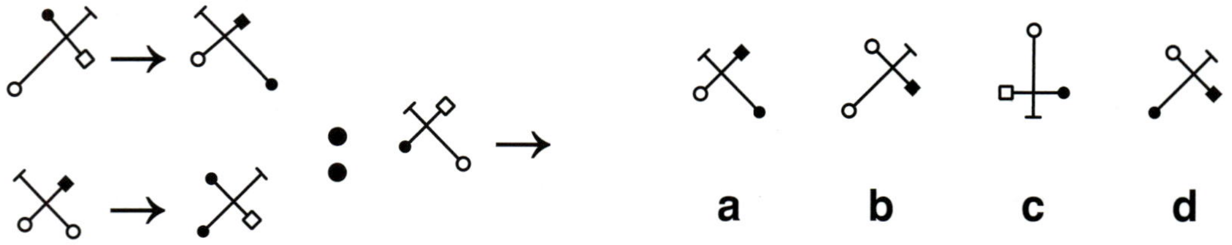

Test Figures

Answer ____

4)

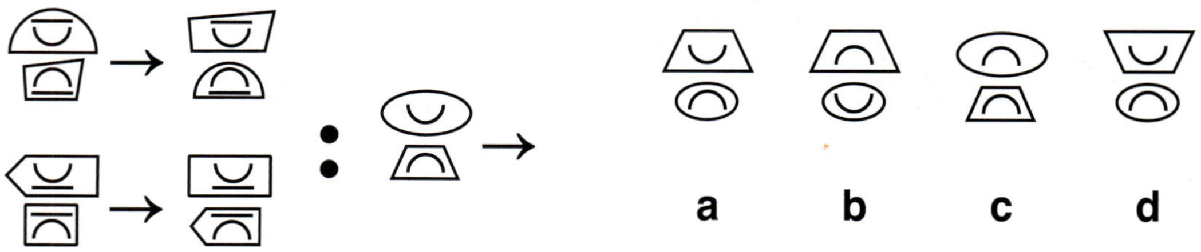

Test Figures

Answer ____

5)

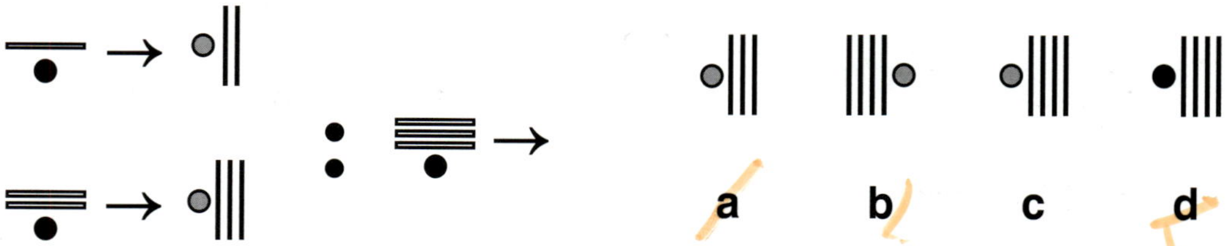

Test Figures

Answer ____

6)

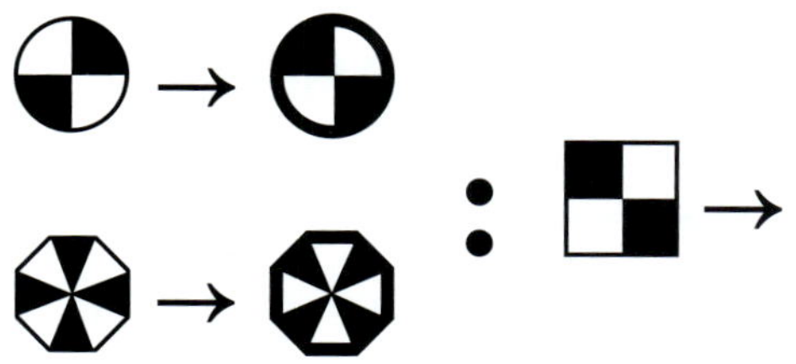

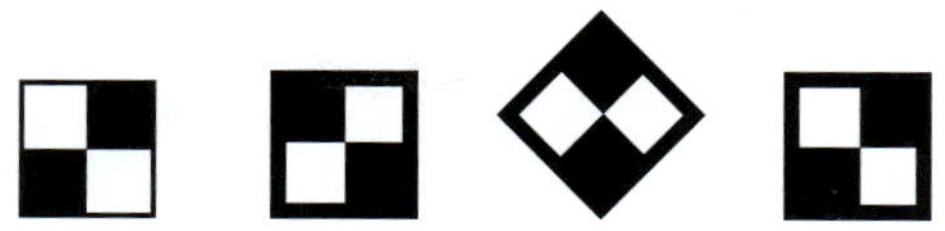

a b c d

Test Figures

Answer d

7)

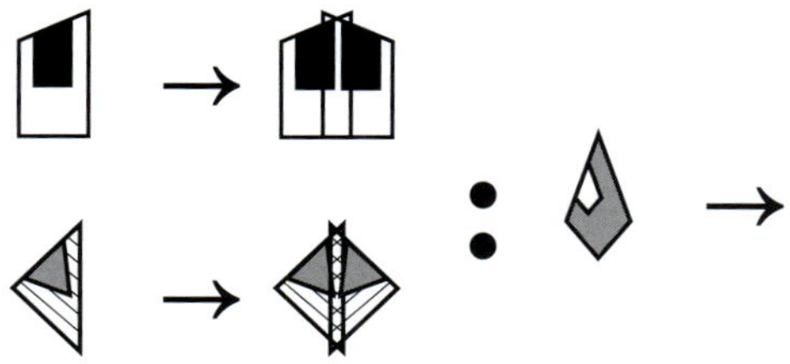

a b c d

Test Figures

Answer a

8)

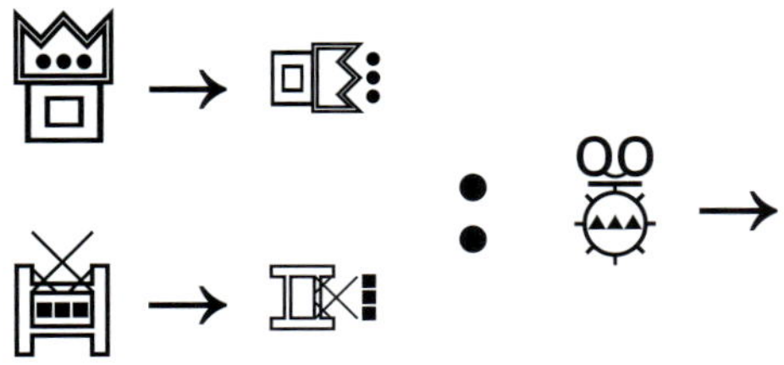

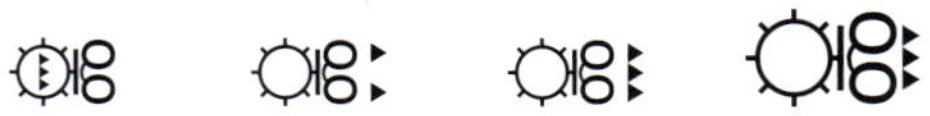

a b c d

Test Figures

Answer c

9)

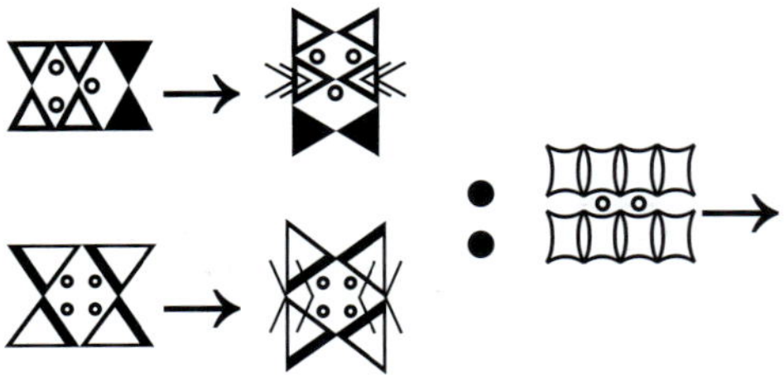

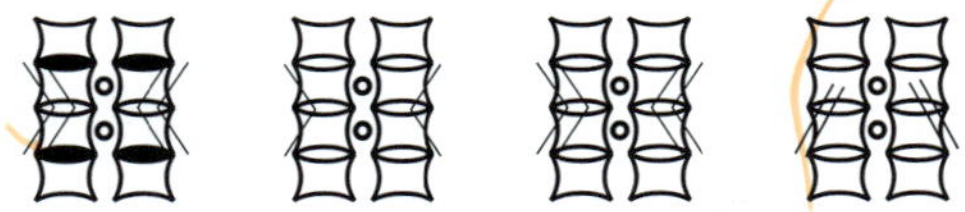

a b c d

Test Figures

Answer c

10)

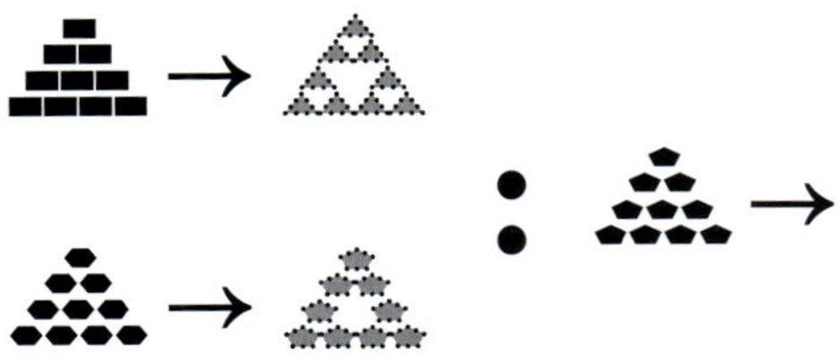

a b c d

Test Figures

Answer b

Score

Chapter Twenty-six
MORE SIMILARITIES

Similarity questions with two test figures are explained in Workbook 2. Similarity questions occur in two further types:

Three Figure Similarities • Four Figure Similarities

More figures means additional similarities can be drawn.

1. Three Figure Similarities

Example: Which figure on the right is most similar to the Test Figures?

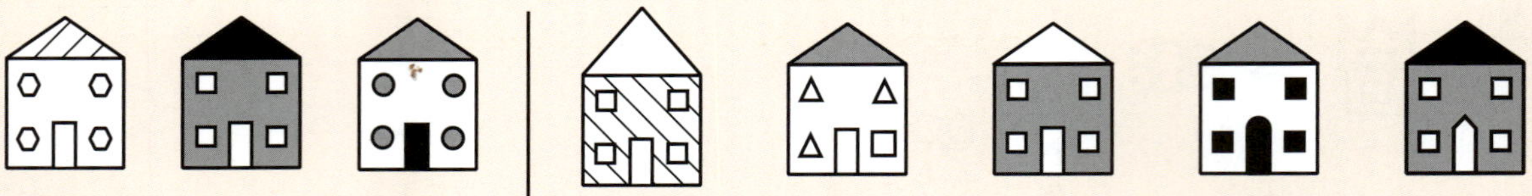

Test Figures — **a** **b** **c** **d** **e**

Step 1 - Establish the similarity rules from the Test Figures.

Test Figures

There are five rules in these Test Figures.

1. Roofs are always the same shape.
2. Doorways are always the same shape.
3. Windows are always the same shape in each house.
4. Walls have either a Grey or White Fill.
5. Windows have either a Grey or White Fill.

Step 2 - Now apply the rules to eliminate the options.

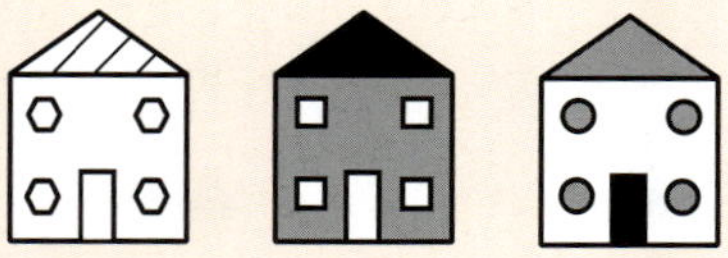

Test Figures

a breaks rules 1 and 4. The roof is the wrong shape and the wall is Shaded.

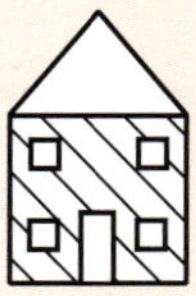

a

b breaks rule 3. The windows are Triangles and not all the same shape.

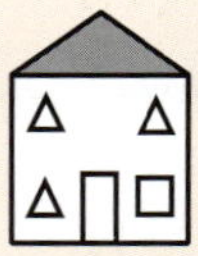

b

d and **e** break rule 2. The door is the wrong shape.

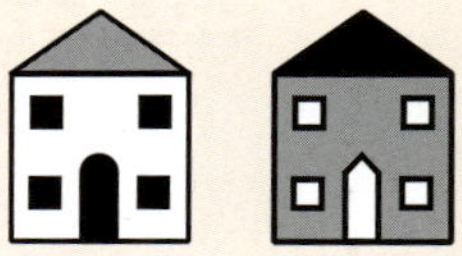

d **e**

c follows all the similarity rules.

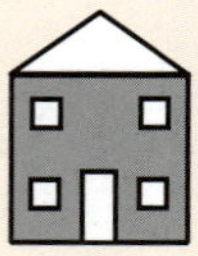

c

c is the correct answer.

Exercise 26: 1

Which figure on the right is most similar to the Test Figures?

1)

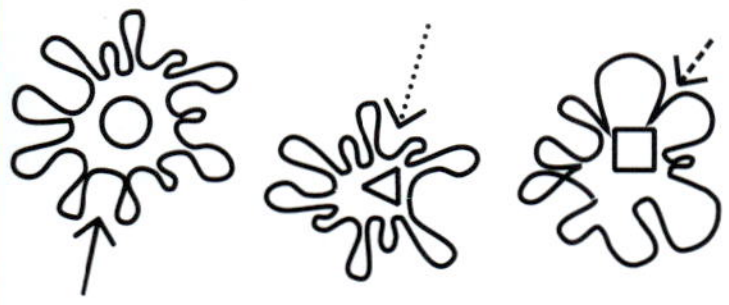

Test Figures

a b c d e

Answer ____

2)

Test Figures

same positions!

a b c d e

Answer c

3)

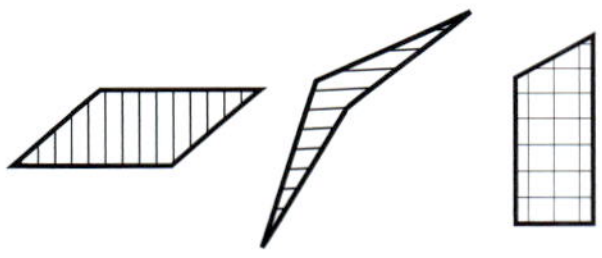

Test Figures

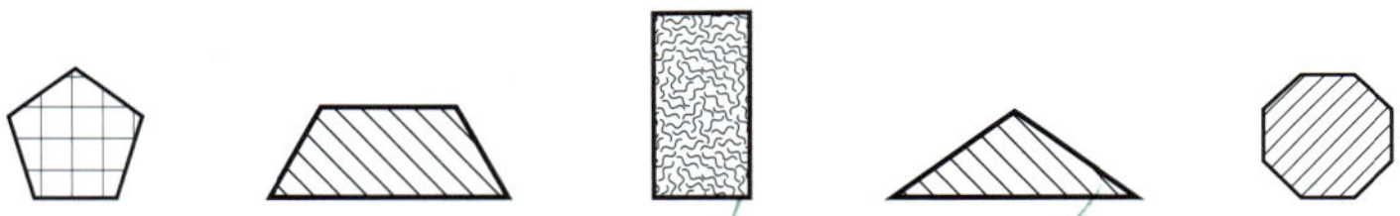

a b c d e

Answer b

4)

Test Figures

a b c d e

Answer B

5)

Test Figures

a b c d e

Answer e

6)

Test Figures

a b c d e

Answer e

7)

Test Figures

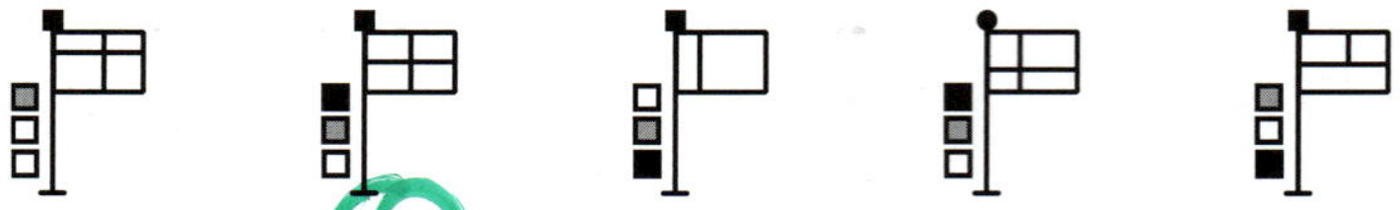

a b c d e

Answer b

8)

Test Figures

a b c d e

Answer d

9)

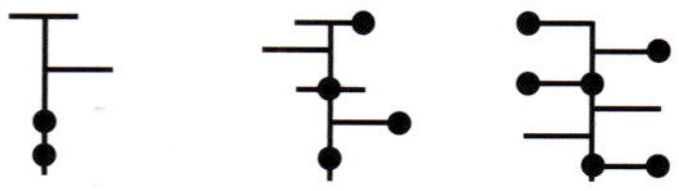

Test Figures

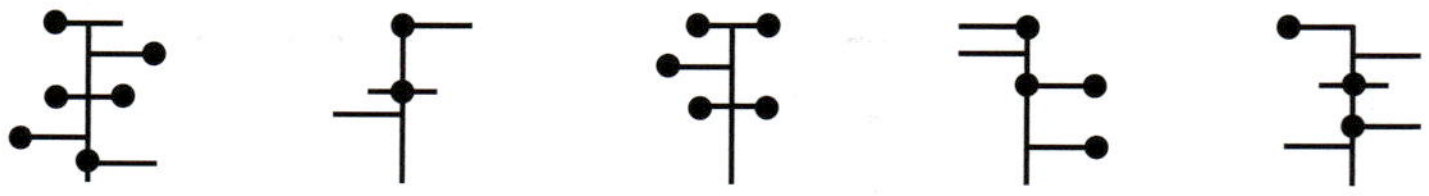

a b c d e

Answer e

10)

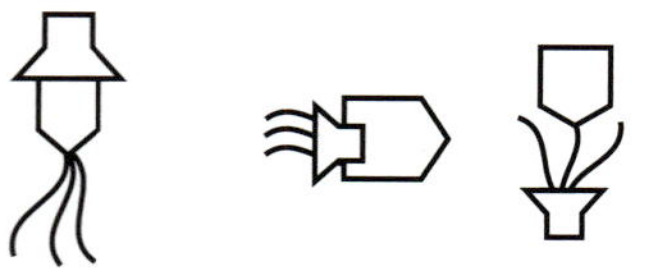

Test Figures

a b c d e

Answer a

Score

2. Four Figure Similarities

Four Figure Similarities is the most complex form of this type of question because more comparisons can be made.

Example: Which figure on the right is most similar to the Test Figures?

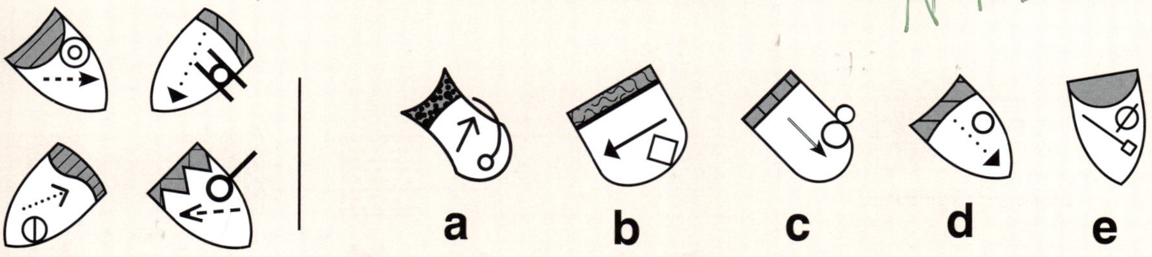

Test Figures

Step 1 - Establish the similarity rules from the Test Figures.

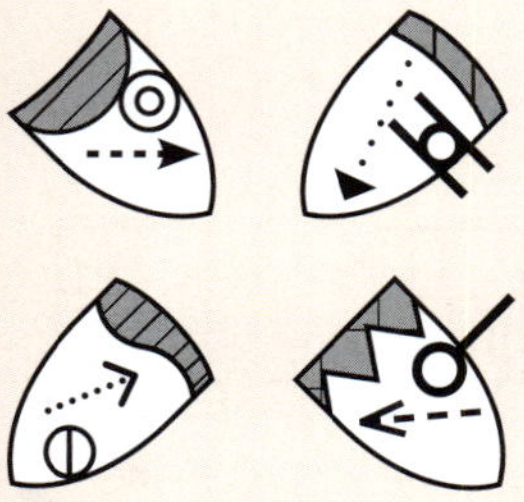

Test Figures

There are six rules in these Test Figures:
1. The exterior shape must be a Shield.
2. Shields slant right or left by 45°.
3. Arrows have a dotted or dashed line.
4. There must be a Circle.
5. There must be a Grey Fill with Line Shading.
6. The Line across the Shield is not Straight.

Step 2 - Now apply the rules to eliminate the options.

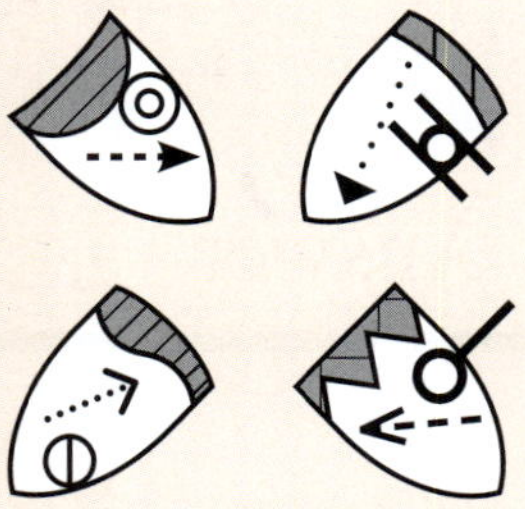

Test Figures

a breaks rules 1, 3 and 5. The exterior shape is a Helmet, the Arrow has a Solid Line and the Grey Fill is Mottled.

a

b and **c** break rules 3 and 4. The Arrows have Solid Lines and there is a Square or external Circle. **b** also breaks rule 2. The Shield does not slant 45°.

b

c

e breaks rules 2 and 3. The Shield does not slant 45° and there is no Arrow.

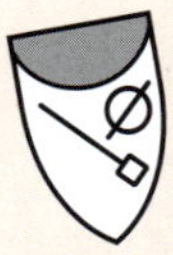

e

d follows all the similarity rules.

d

d is the correct answer.

Exercise 26: 2

Which figure on the right is most similar to the Test Figures?

1)

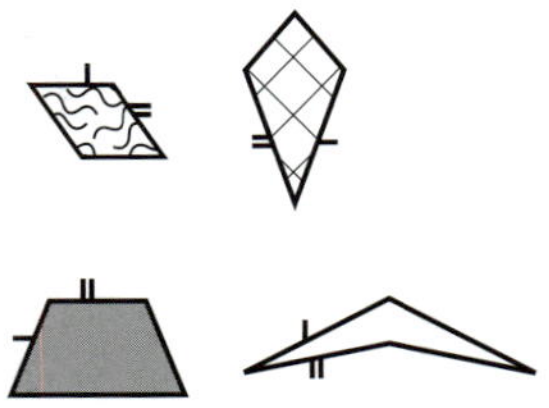

Test Figures

a b c d e

Answer ____

2)

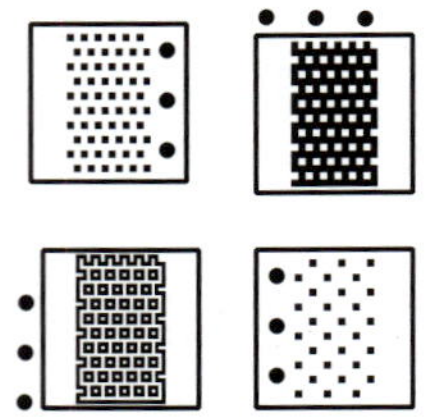

Test Figures

a b c d e

Answer ____

3)

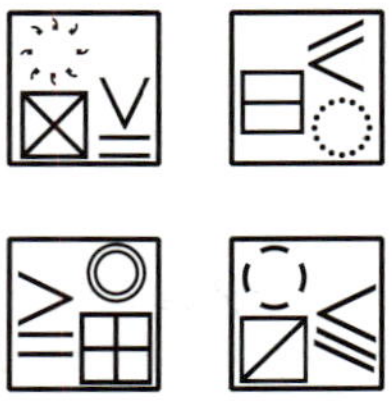

Test Figures

a b c d e

Answer ____

4)

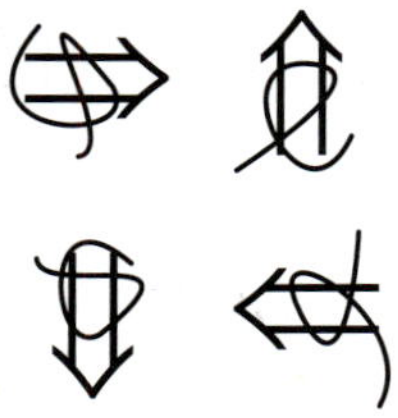

Test Figures

a b c d e

Answer ____

5)

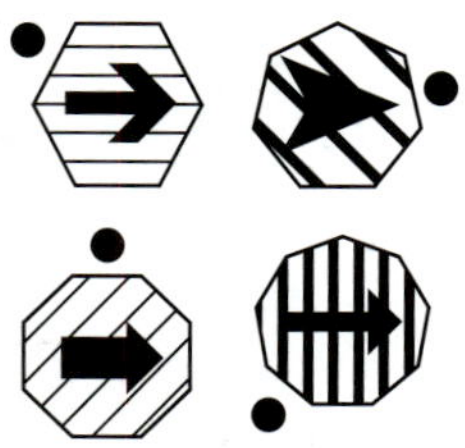

Test Figures

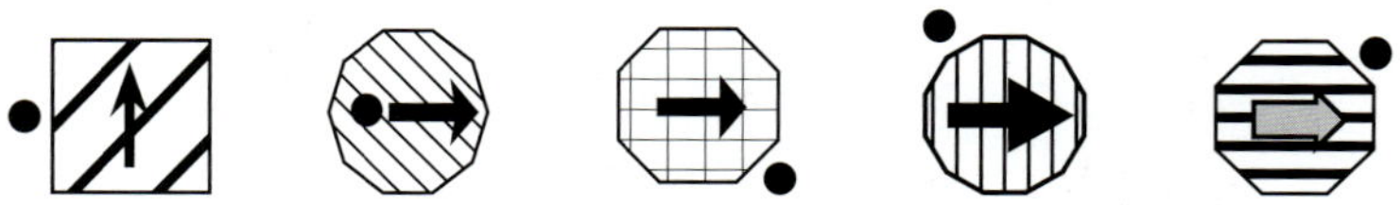

a b c d e

Answer ____

6)

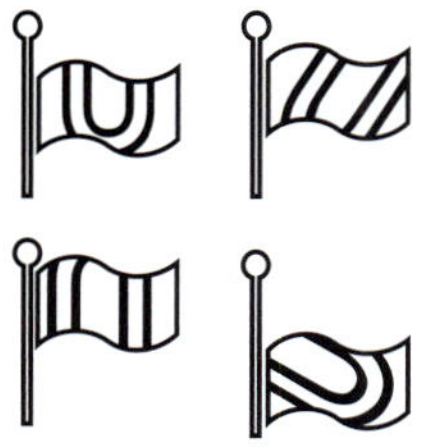

Test Figures

a b c d e

Answer ____

7)

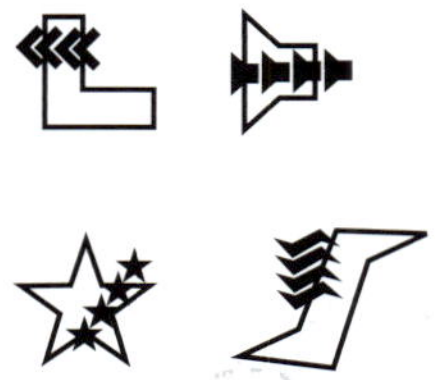

Test Figures

a b c d e

Answer ____

8)

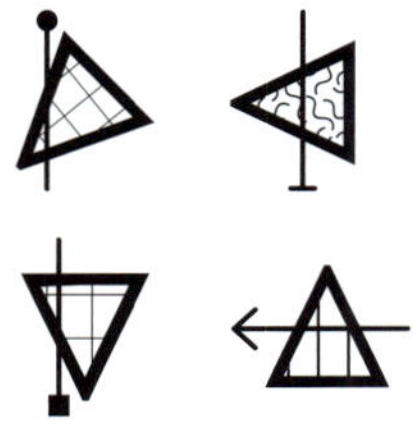

Test Figures

a b c d e

Answer ____

9)

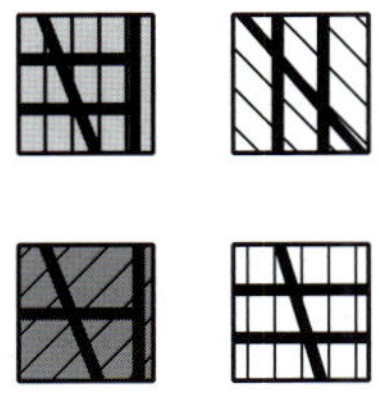

Test Figures

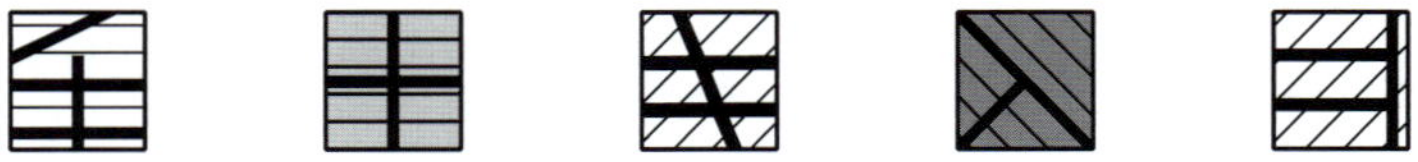

a b c d e

Answer ____

10)

Test Figures

a b c d e

Answer ____

Score

Chapter Twenty-seven
MORE MATRICES

Matrices with 4 and 9 squares are explained in Workbook 2.
16 Square Matrix • 25 Square Matrix
Hexagon Matrix • Other Matrix Types
More squares in the matrix increase the question complexity.

1. 16 Square Matrix

Example: Which figure completes the matrix?

a b c d e

Step 1 - Establish the matrix rules.

There are five rules to this matrix:
1. Columns and rows alternate Black/White Fills.
2. Crosses are completed with Diagonal Lines.
3. Same shapes in opposite corners rotate 180°.
4. Other outer row/column shapes reflect.
5. Four shapes in the middle must all be different.

Step 2 - Now apply the rules to eliminate the options.

b and **d** break rules 2 and 4. The shapes are incorrect and the Line is missing or in the wrong place.

b

d

e breaks rule 1. The shape should be White and the Line is the wrong place.

e

a breaks rule 1. The Diamond should have a White Fill.

a

c follows all the matrix rules.

c

c completes the matrix.

Exercise 27: 1 Which figure completes the matrix?

1)

∞	8	≈	Ω
Ω	≈	8	∞
≈	Ω		8
8	∞	Ω	≈

a	b	c	d	e
Ω	≈	8	∞	≈

Answer ____

2)

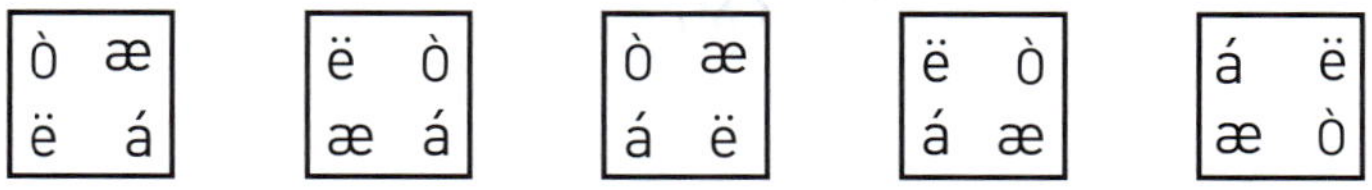

a b c d e

Answer ____

3)

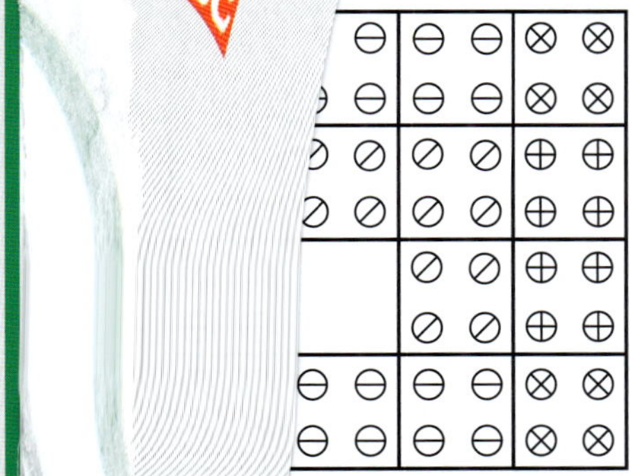

a b c d e

Answer ____

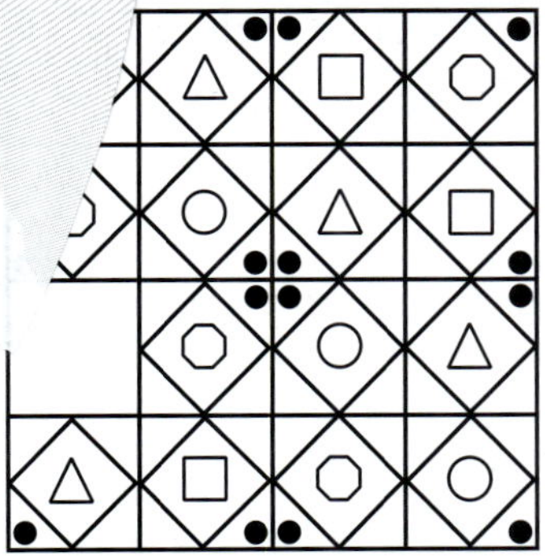

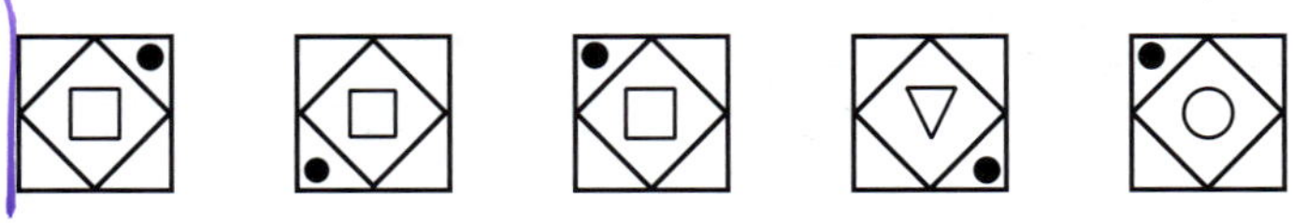

a b c d e

Answer ____

5)

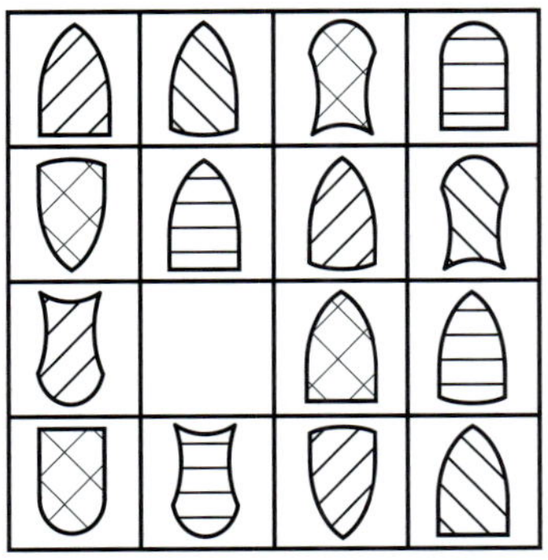

a b c d e

Answer ____

6) 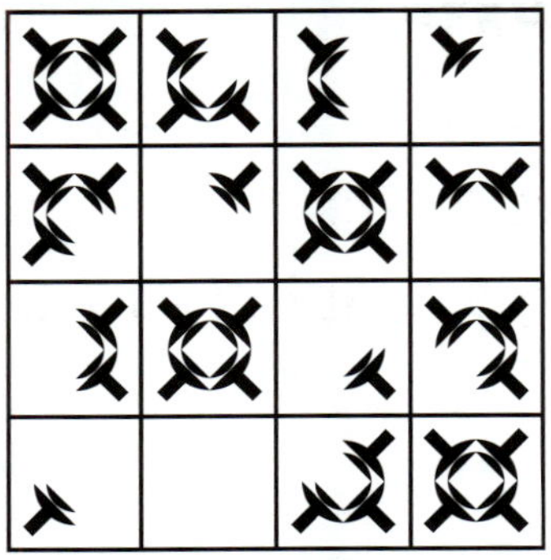

a b c d e

Answer ____

7) 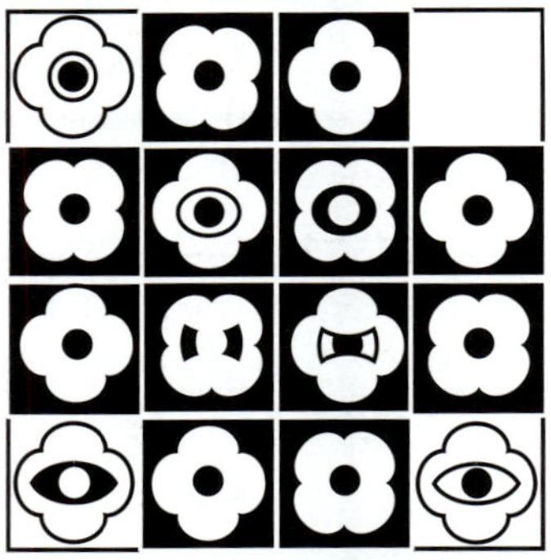

a b c d e

Answer ____

8) 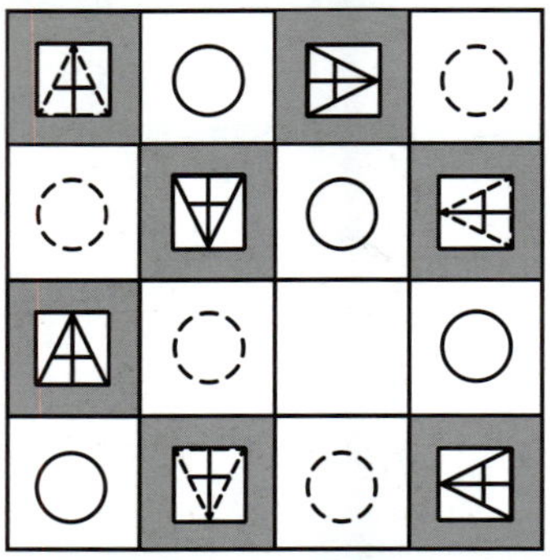

a b c d e

Answer ____

9) 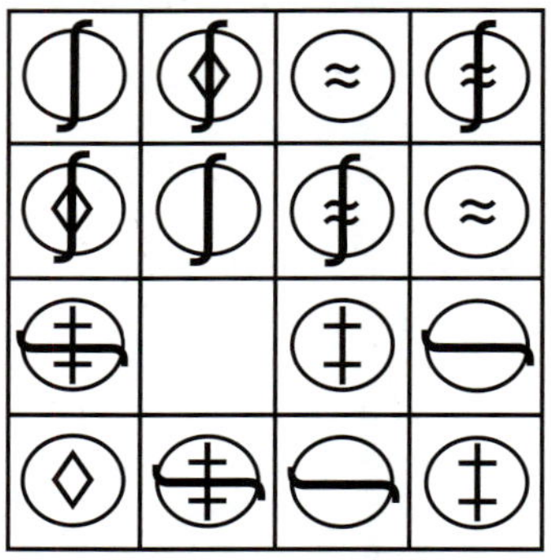

a b c d e

Answer ____

10) 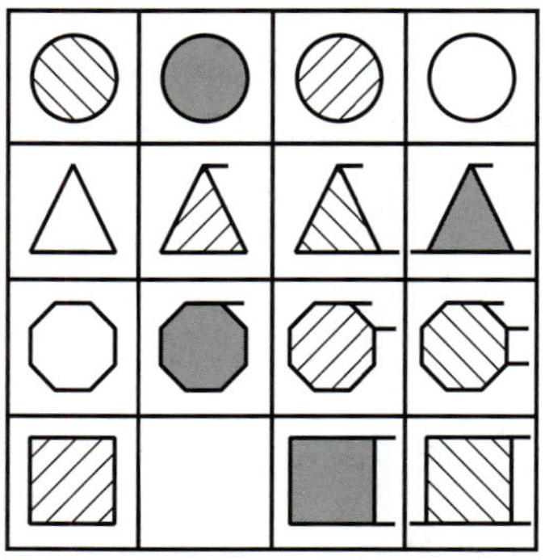

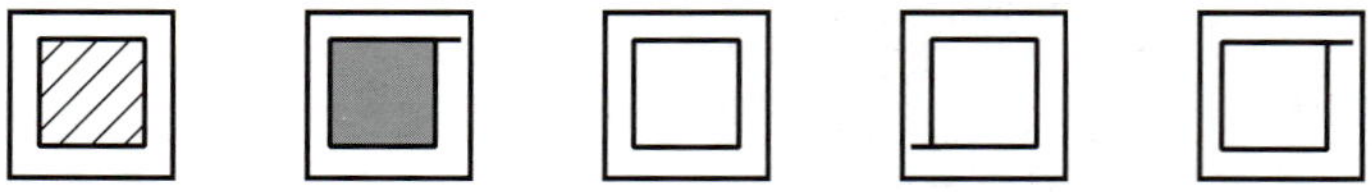

a b c d e

Answer ____ **Score**

2. 25 Square Matrix

A **25 Square Matrix** can be the most complex NVR question to solve because it can incorporate a large number of rules.

Example: Which figure completes the matrix?

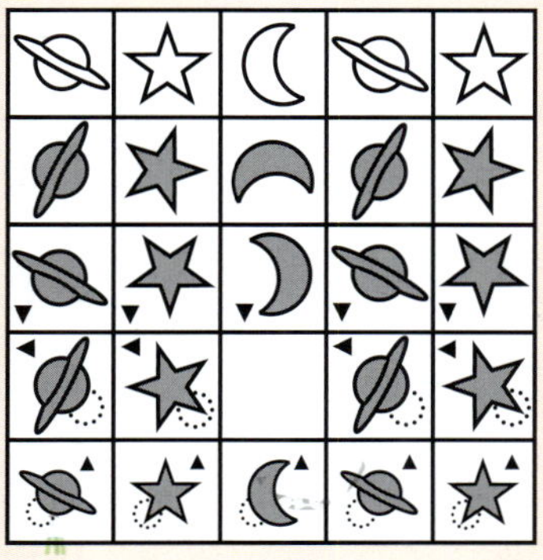

a b c d e

Step 1 - Establish the matrix rules.

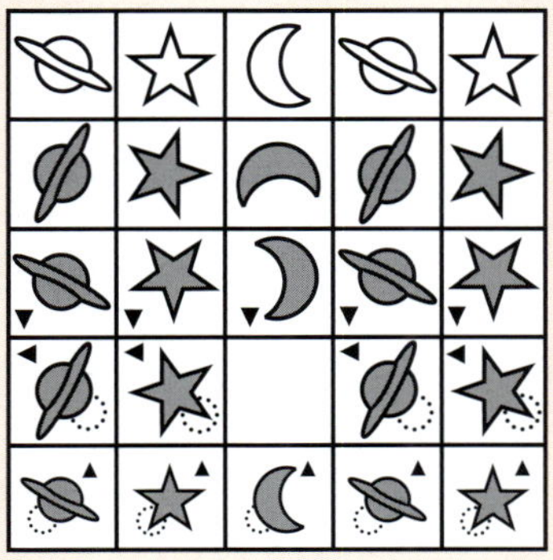

There are six rules in this matrix:
1. Each column only has one type of shape.
2. Row 1 shapes have White Fills/rows 2-5 have Grey Fills.
3. All shapes rotate 90º Anticlockwise by column.
4. Triangles appear on the left in rows 3-5.
5. A Dotted Circle appears in row 4 to the right.
6. The figure reduces in size in row 5.

Step 2 - Now apply the rules to eliminate the options.

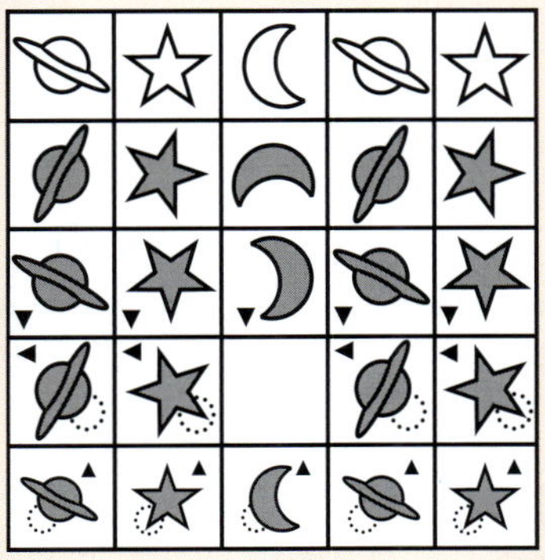

a breaks rules 1, 2 and 5. The shape and fill are wrong. There is no Dotted Circle.

a

c breaks rules 3, 4 and 5. The shape rotation is incorrect, the Triangle is on the wrong side and there is no Dotted Circle.

c

d breaks rule 3. The Triangle is in the wrong position.

d

e breaks rule 3. The Dotted Circle is on the wrong side.

e

b follows all the matrix rules.

b

b completes the matrix.

Exercise 27: 2 Which figure completes the matrix?

1) 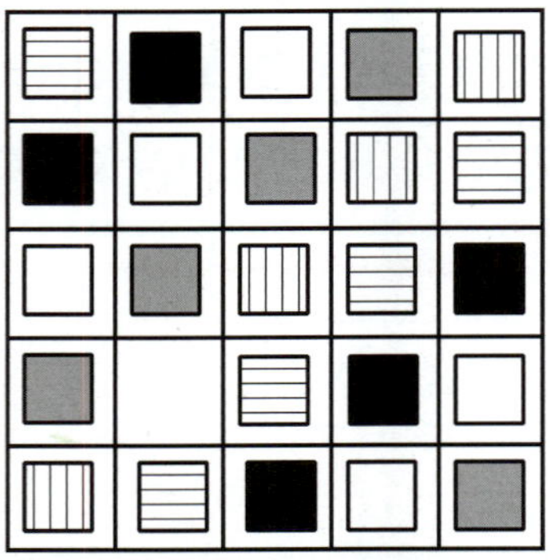

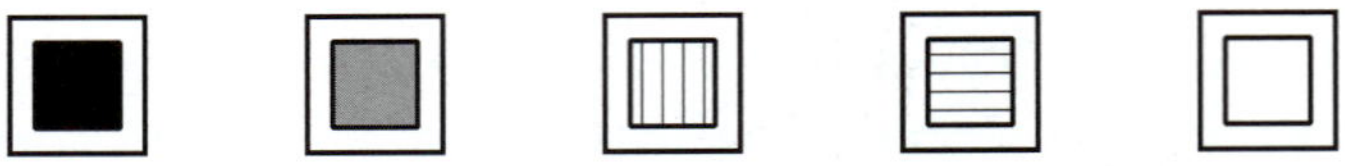

a b c d e

Answer c

2) 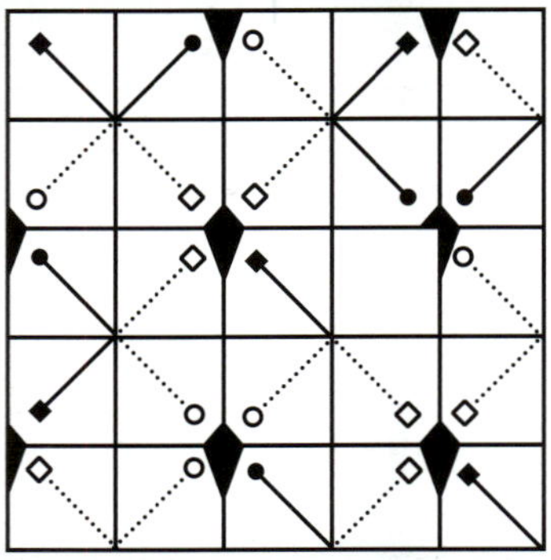

a b c d e

Answer d

3) 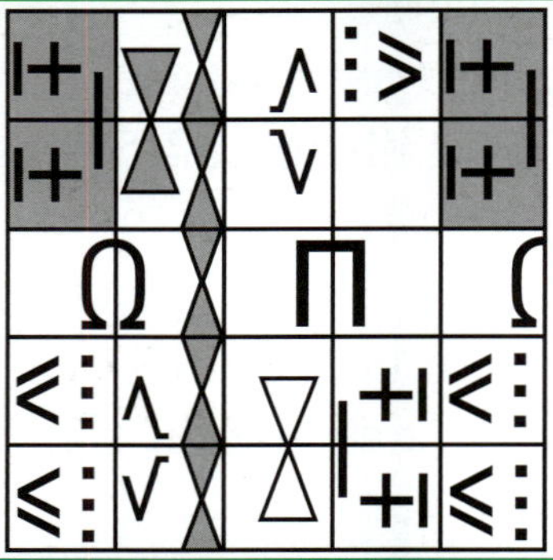

a b c d e

Answer a

4) 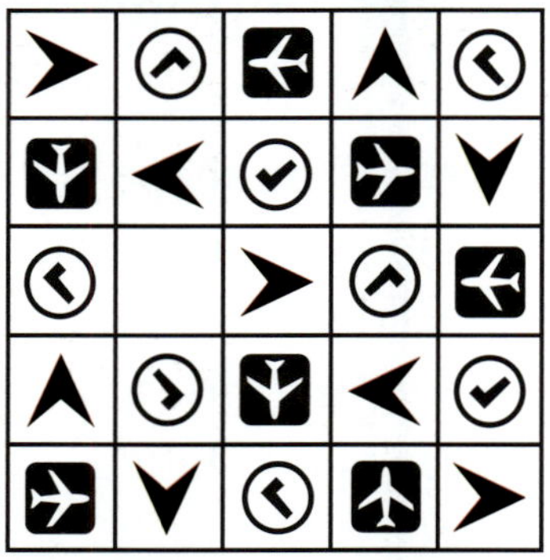

a b c d e

Answer a

5) 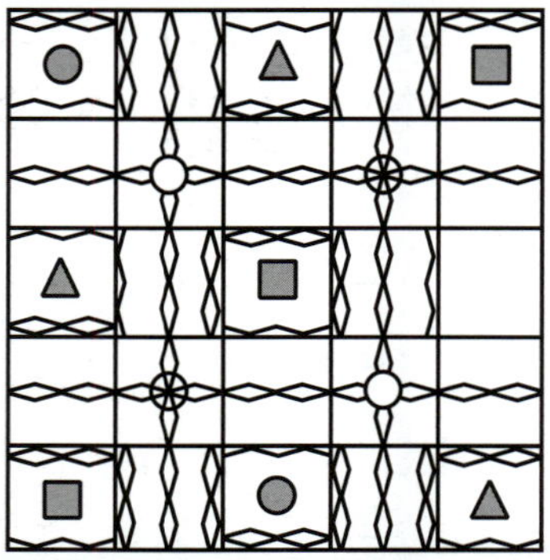

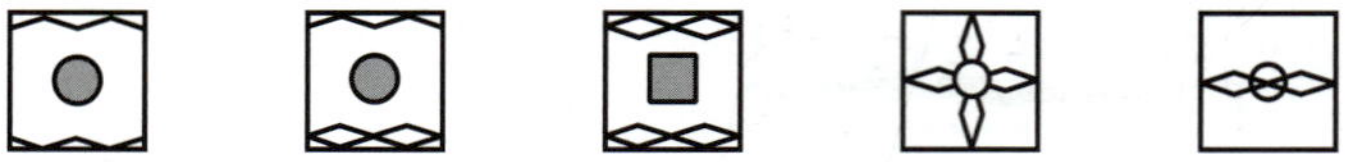

a b c d e

Answer b

6) 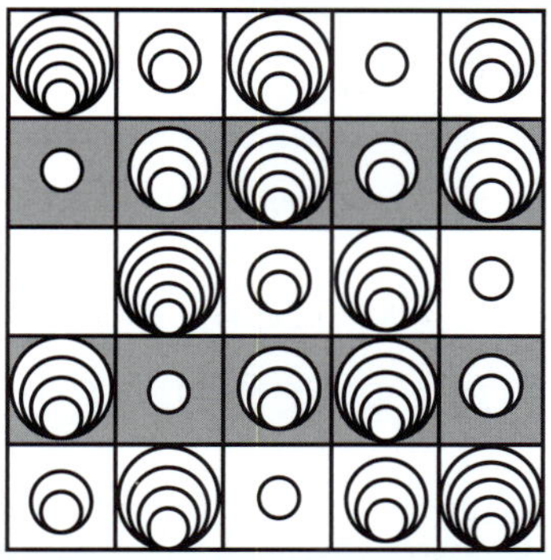

a b c d e

Answer ____

7) 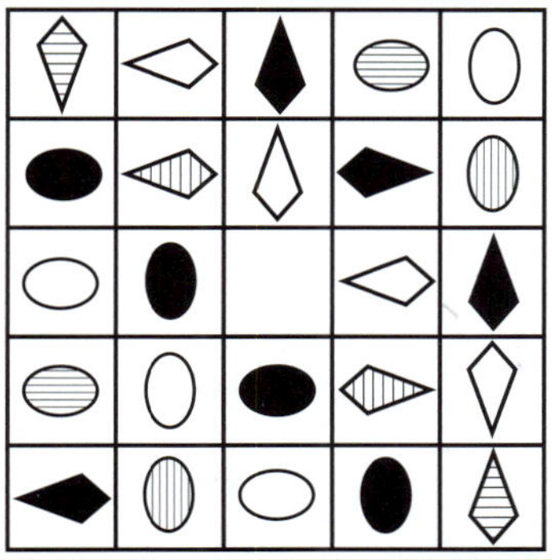

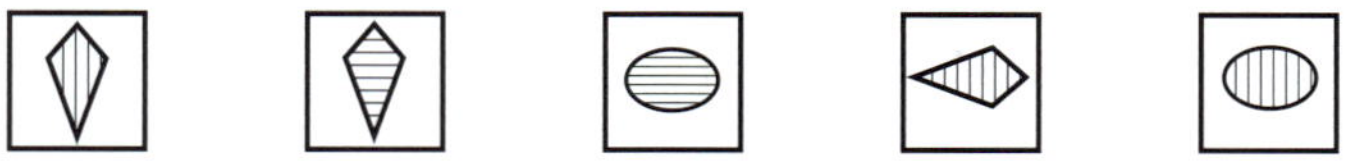

a b c d e

Answer ____

8) 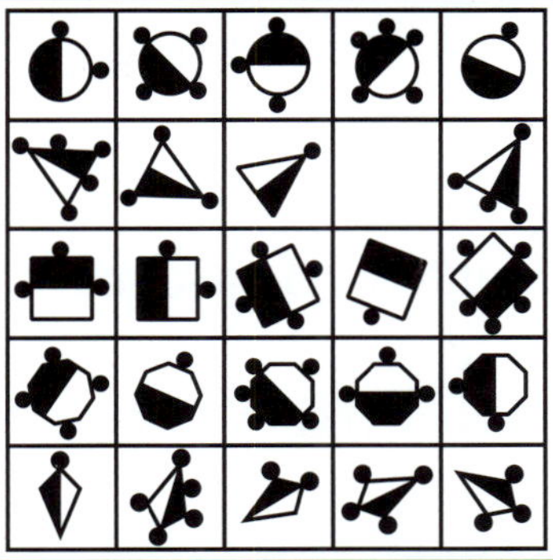

a b c d e

Answer ____

9) 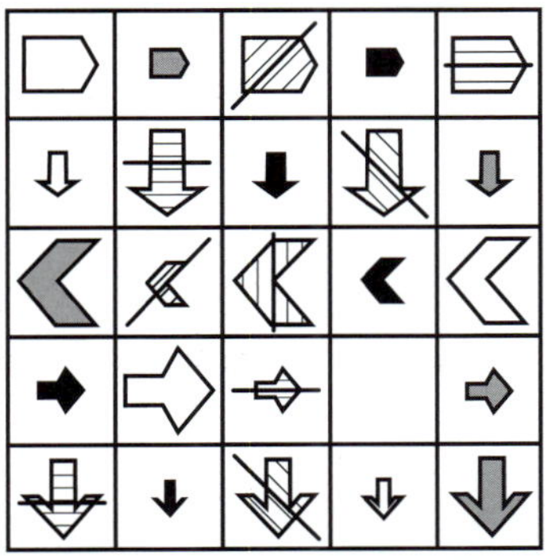

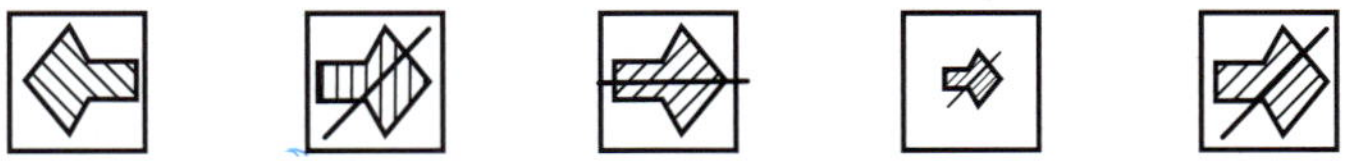

a b c d e

Answer ____

10) 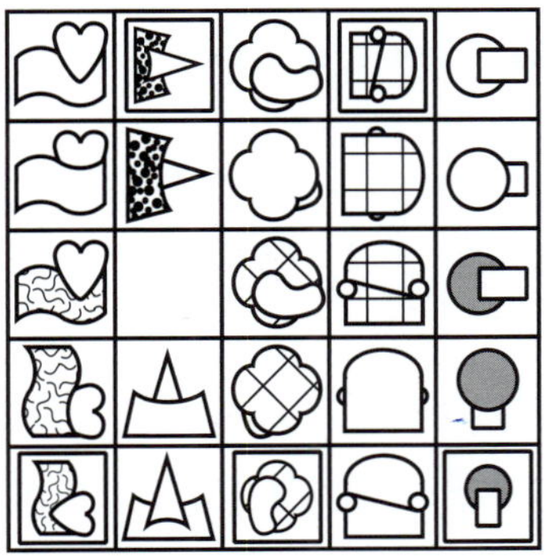

a b c d e

Answer ____

Score 

3. Hexagon Matrix

A **Hexagon Matrix** is a variant form that creates different rule combinations from Square Matrices. For example, it is possible to create a series question from seven hexagons which can start at any point around the central hexagon.

Example: Which figure completes the matrix?

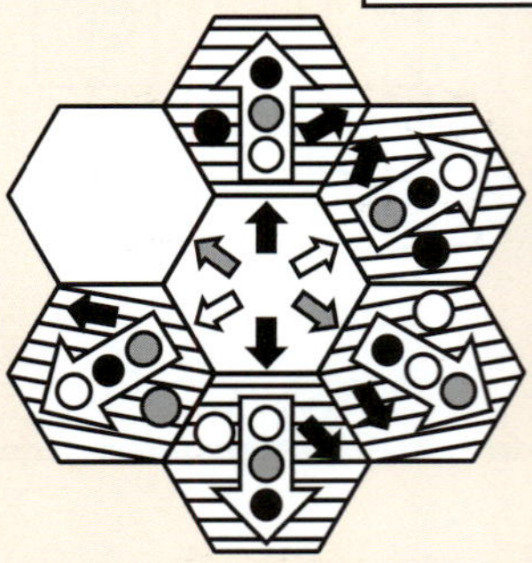

a b c d e

Step 1 - Establish the matrix rules.

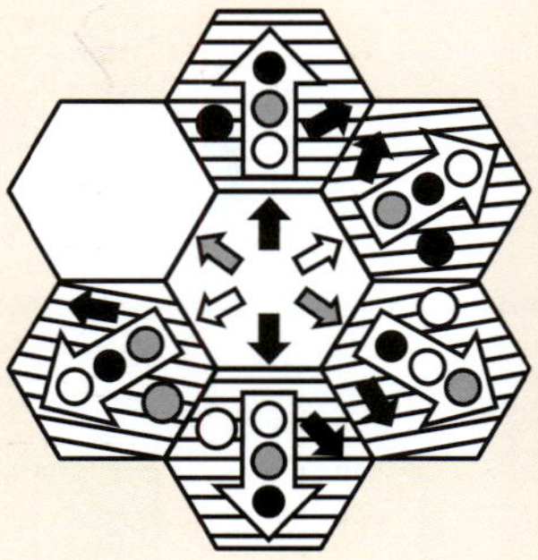

There are six rules in this matrix:

1. Shading: Horizontal, Left Slant x2, Horizontal, Right Slant x2, Horizontal, etc.
2. The Circles within the Arrows alternate - Black, White, Grey, Black, etc.
3. Black Fill Arrow alternates Right, Left, Right, etc.
4. Exterior Circle alternates Left, Right, Left, etc.
5. Exterior Circle fills: Black, Black, White, White, Grey, etc.
6. Arrow fills in central hexagon match Circle fill at point of Arrow.

Step 2 - Now apply the rules to eliminate the options.

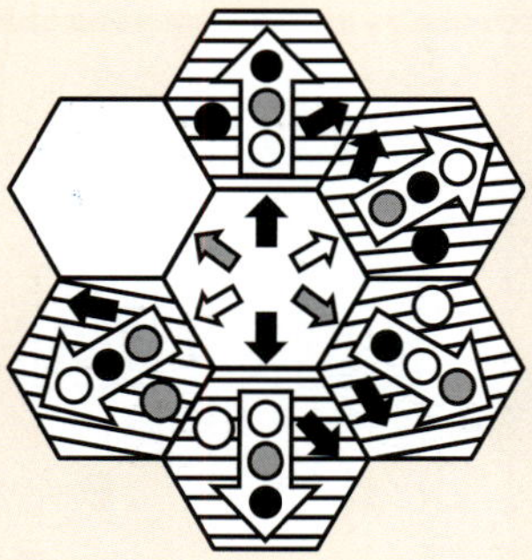

b breaks rules 1, 3 and 5. The shading is wrong. The Circle fill and position are wrong. There is no Black Fill Arrow.

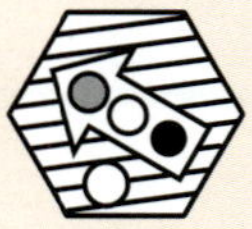

b

e breaks rules 1 and 2. The shading and two Circle fills are wrong.

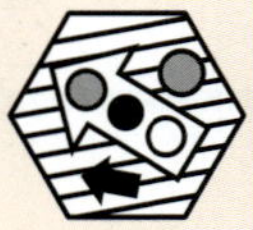

e

d breaks rules 3, 4 and 5. There are two Arrows and no Circles.

d

c breaks rules 1, 2, 3, 4, 5 and 6.

c

a follows all the matrix rules.

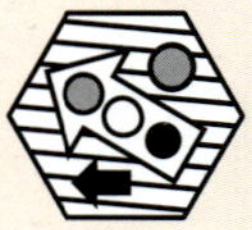

a

a completes the matrix.

Exercise 27: 3

Which figure completes the hexagon matrix?

1) 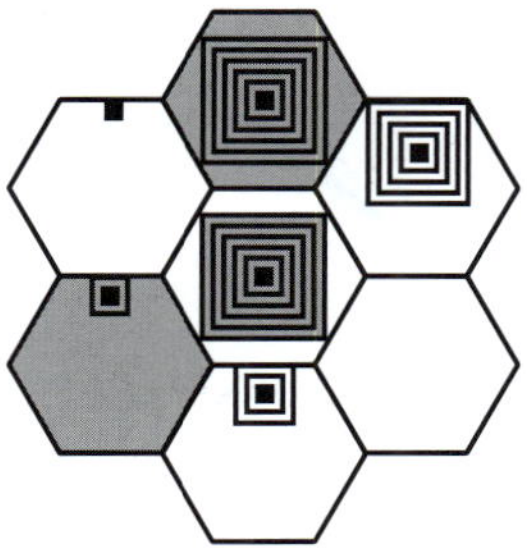

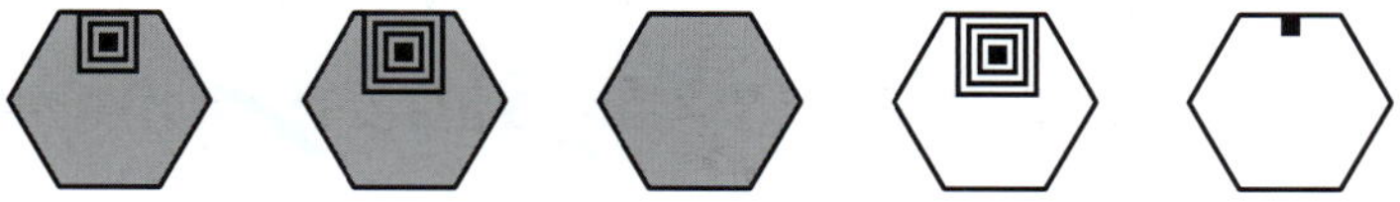

a b c d e

Answer b

2) 

a b c d e

Answer e

3) 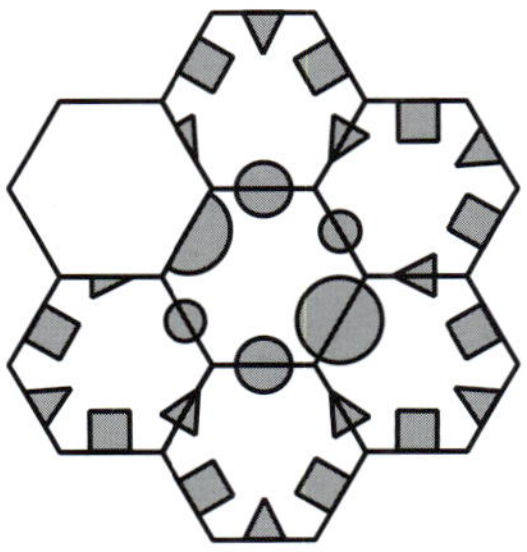

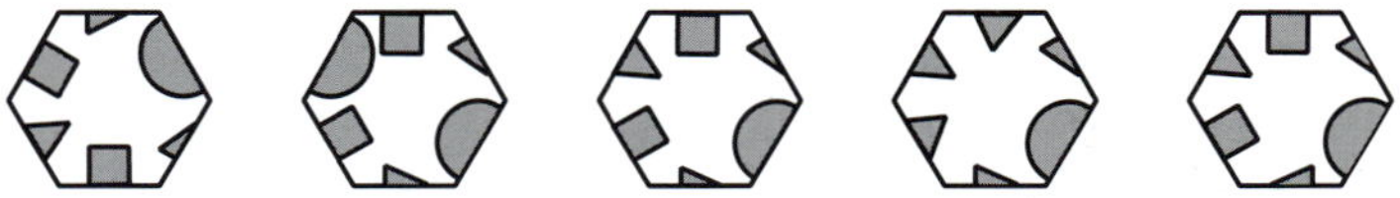

a b c d e

Answer c

4) 

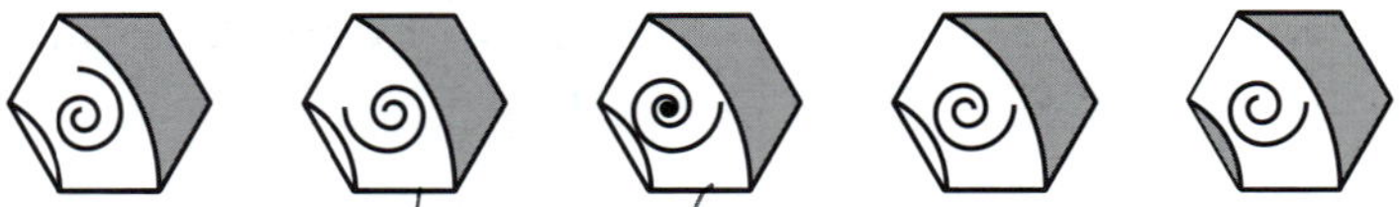

a b c d e

Answer d

5) 

a b c d e

Answer a

6) 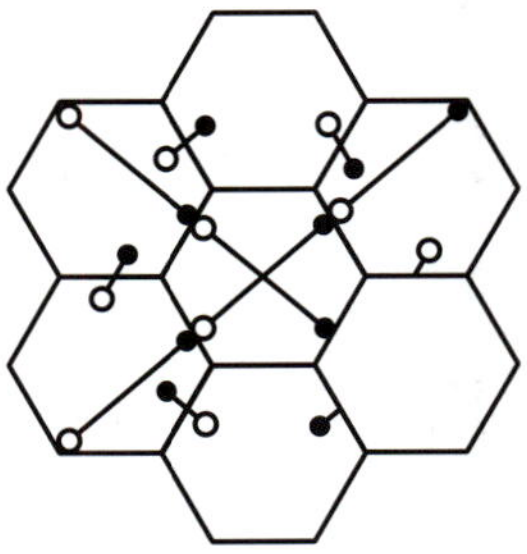

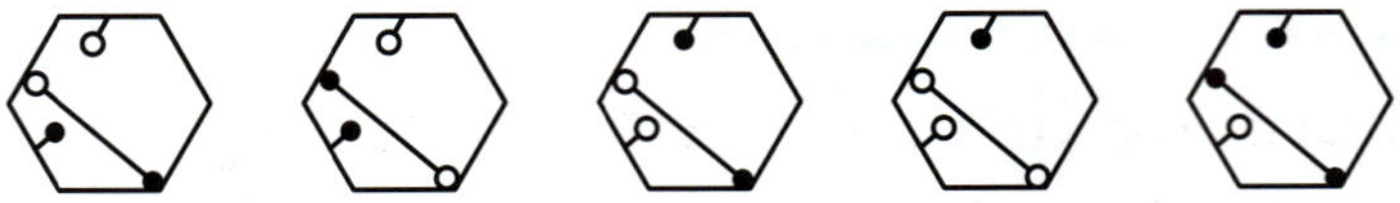

a b c d e

Answer c

7) 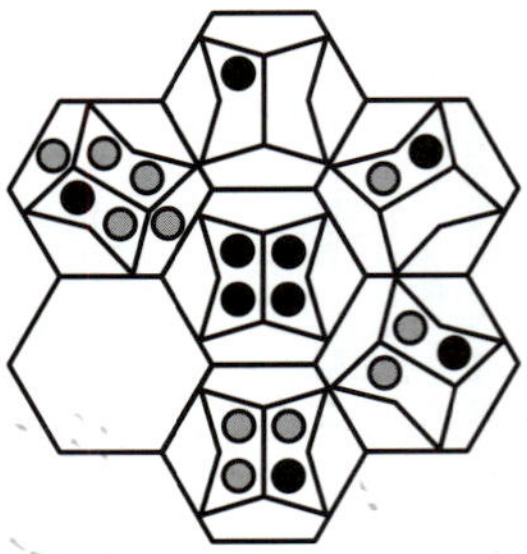

a b c d e

Answer e

8) 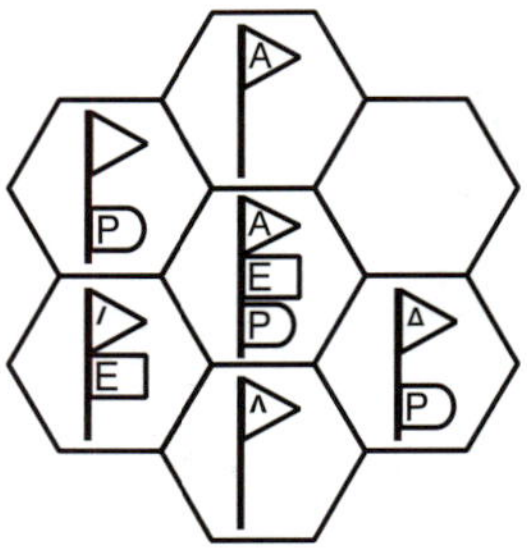

a b c d e

Answer ____

9) 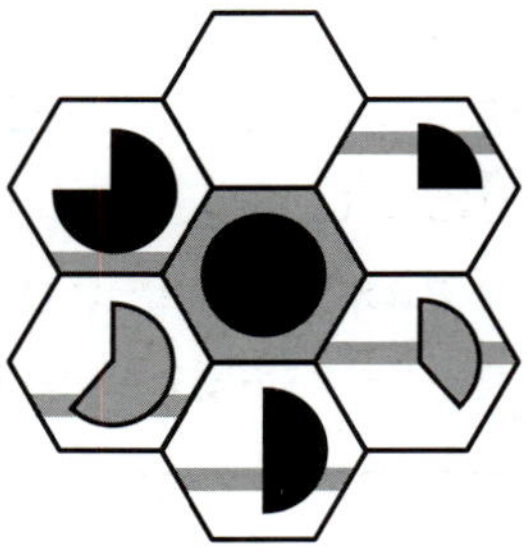

a b c d e

Answer d

10) 

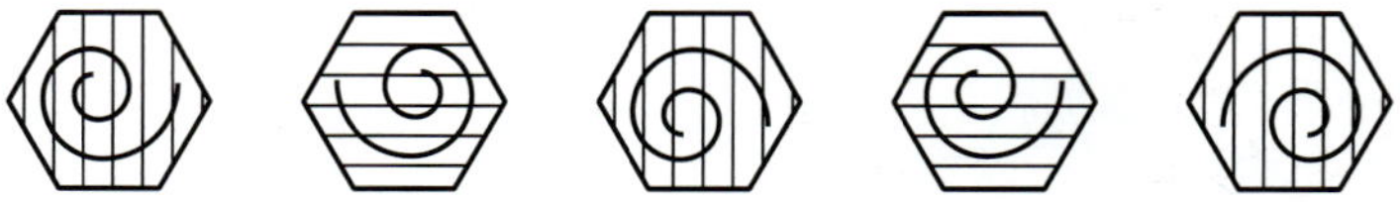

a b c d e

Answer a

Score

4. Other Matrix Types

There are three **Other Matrix Types** that also create the possibility of different rule combinations:
Cross Matrix • Diamond Matrix • Staggered Matrix

a. Cross Matrix

Example: Which figure completes the matrix?

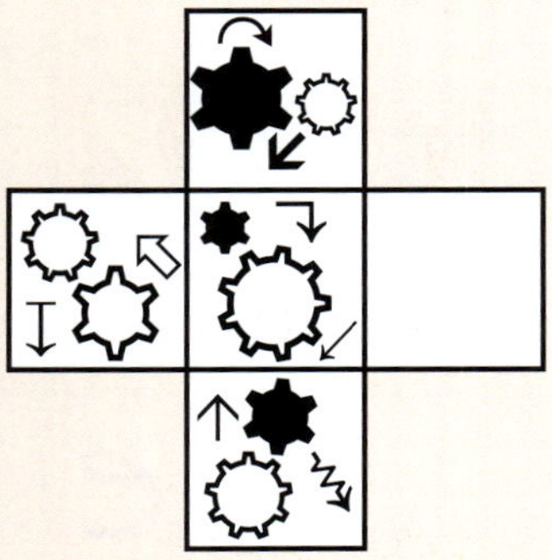

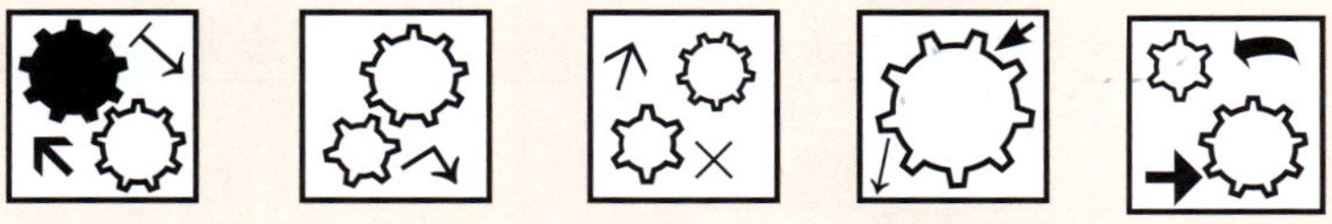

a **b** **c** **d** **e**

Step 1 - Establish the matrix rules.

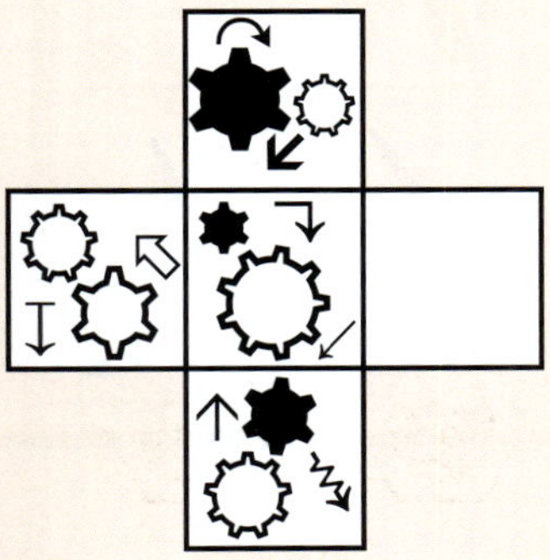

There are five rules in this matrix:

1. There must be one of each type of Sprocket.
2. The Six-pronged Sprocket reduces in size in an Anticlockwise movement around the Cross.
3. The Nine-pronged Sprocket increases in size in an Anticlockwise movement around the Cross.
4. Arrows alternate between a Clockwise flow and an Anticlockwise flow around the Cross.
5. The Six-pronged Sprocket alternates between a Black and White Fill Anticlockwise around the Cross.

Step 2 - Now apply the rules to eliminate the options.

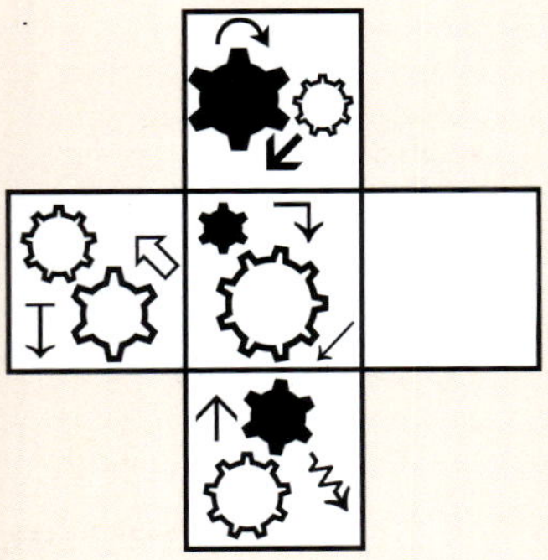

a breaks rules 1, 4 and 5. The Sprockets are the same, have the wrong fills and the Arrows point the wrong way.

a

c breaks rules 3 and 4. The Nine-pronged Sprocket is too small and there is only one Arrow.

c

b breaks rule 4 as there is only one Arrow.

b

d breaks rule 1 as there is only one Sprocket.

d

e follows all the matrix rules.

e

e completes the matrix.

Exercise 27: 4a Which figure completes the matrix?

1)

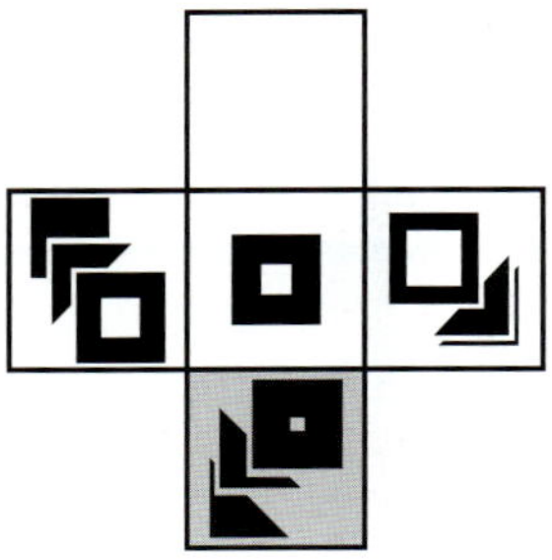

a b c d e

Answer b

2)

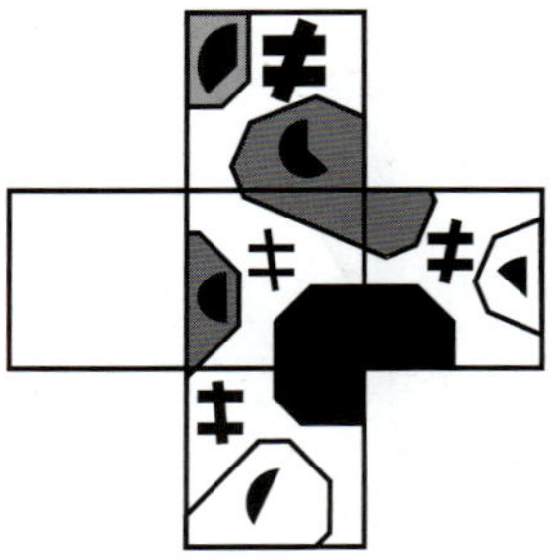

a b c d e

Answer e

3)

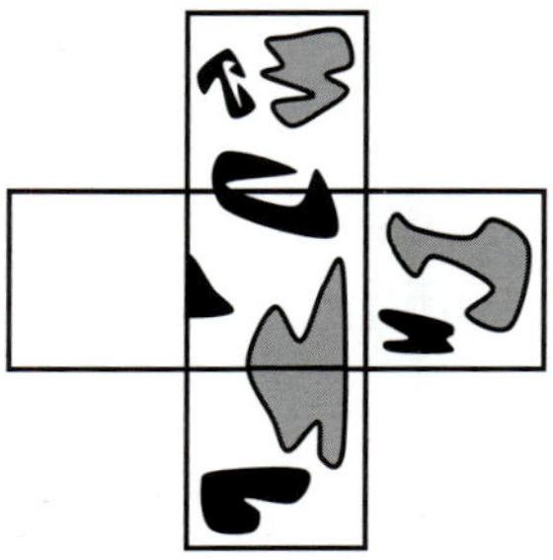

a b c d e

Answer c

b. Diamond Matrix

Example: Which figure completes the matrix?

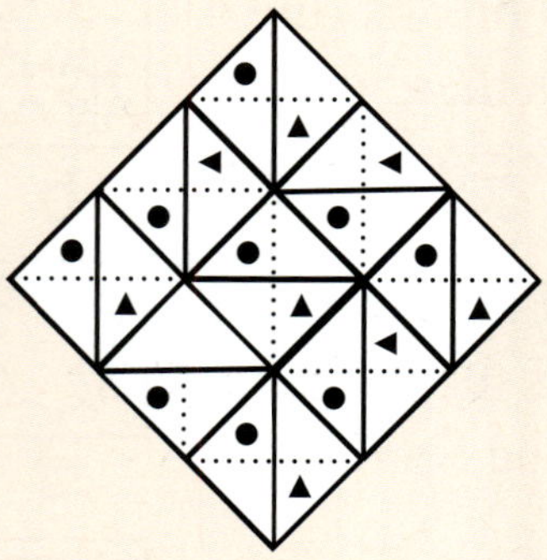

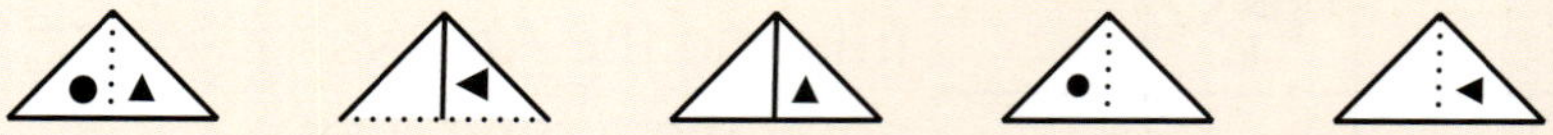

a b c d e

Step 1 - Establish the matrix rules.

There are four rules in this matrix:

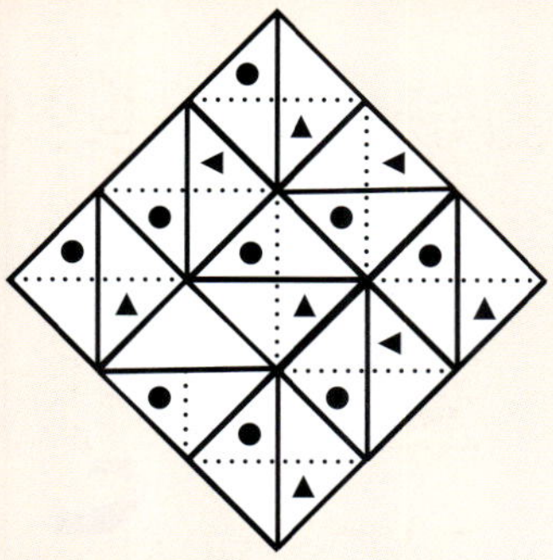

1. There must be a Black Fill Triangle diagonally opposite to the Circle in every square.
2. There is a Dotted Line across each square.
3. There is a Solid Line across each square.
4. The Triangle alternates pointing up and left by row.

Step 2 - Now apply the rules to eliminate the options.

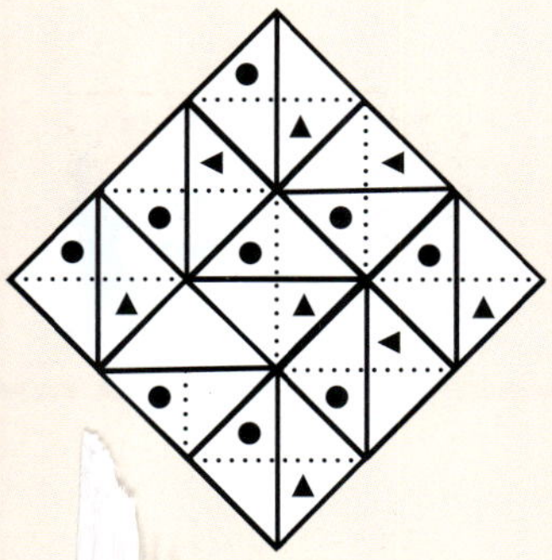

a breaks rules 1 and 4. There should be no Circle and the Triangle points the wrong way.

a

b breaks rules 2 and 3. The Lines are round the wrong way.

b

c breaks rules 2 and 4. There should be a Dotted Line and the Triangle points the wrong way.

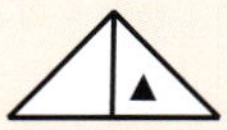

c

d breaks rule 1. There should be a Triangle and not a Circle.

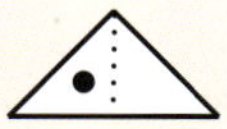

d

e follows all the matrix rules.

e

e completes the matrix.

Exercise 27: 4b Which figure completes the matrix?

4)

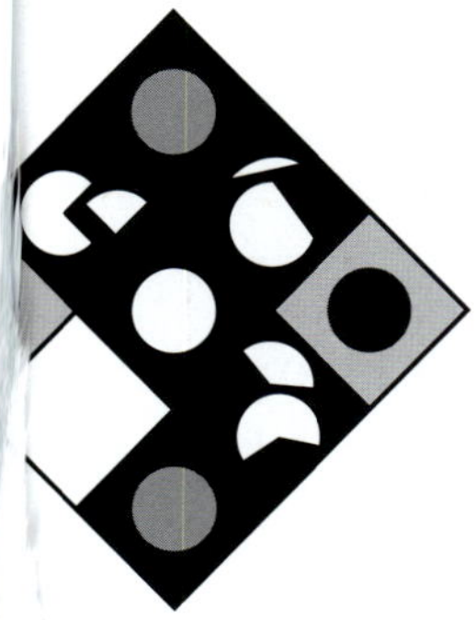

a **b** **c** **d** **e**

Answer b

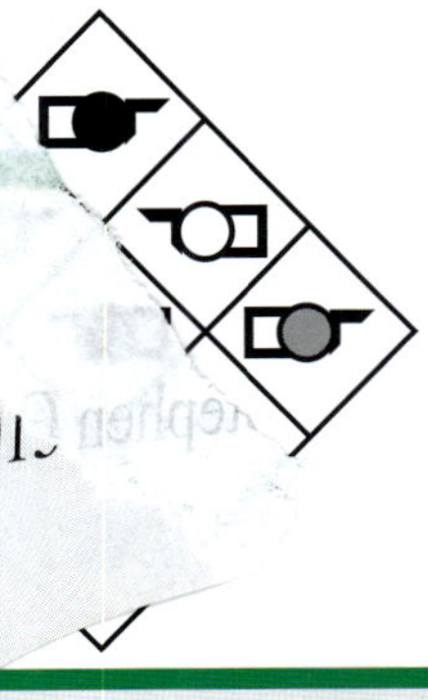

a **b** **c** **d** **e**

Answer e

6)

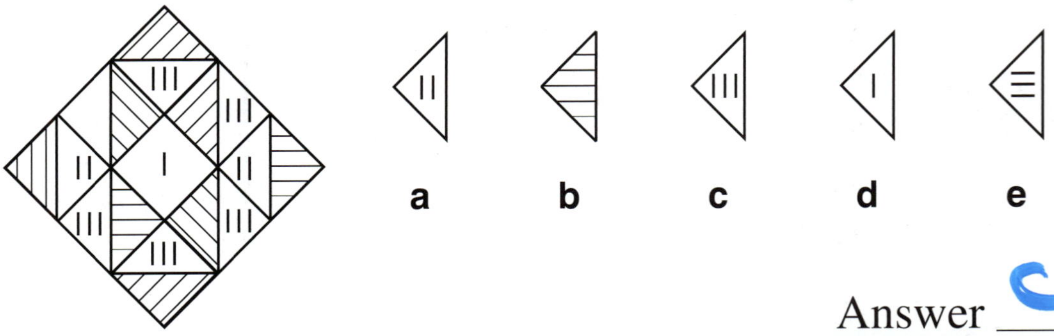

Answer c

7)

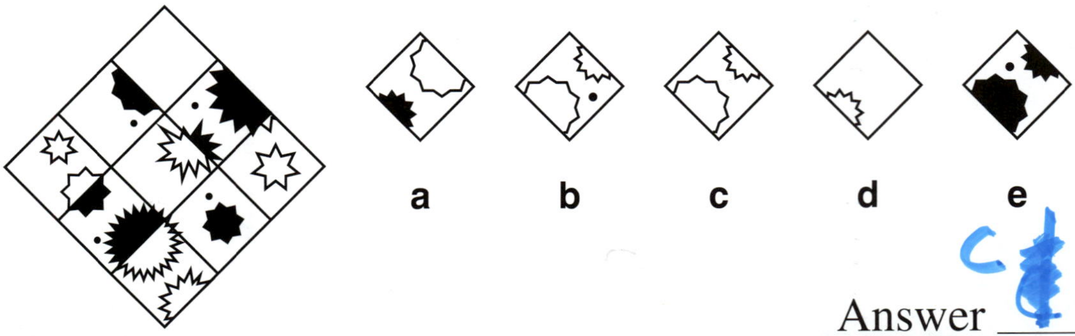

Answer c

c. Staggered Matrix

Example: Which figure completes the matrix?

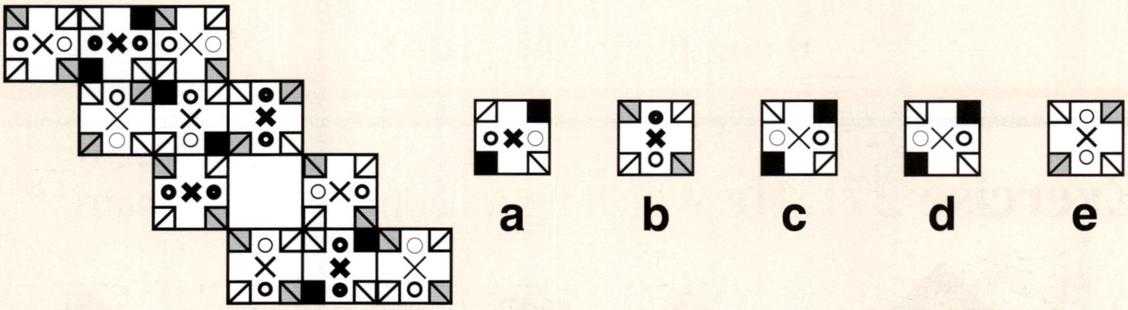

Step 1 - Establish the matrix rules.

There are five rules in this matrix:

1. Heavy, medium and light Line thicknesses of Cross and Circles must occur in each row.
2. Orientation of Cross and Circles alternate per row - Horizontal, Vertical, etc.
3. Small Square Fills alternate - Grey/White, White/Black, Grey/White, etc.
4. Diagonal Lines in small Squares must point towards centre Cross.
5. Fills in small Squares alternate - Diagonally left, Diagonally right, Diagonally left, etc.

Step 2 - Now apply the rules to eliminate the options.

b breaks rules 1, 2, 3 and 5. The Cross/Circle type and Squares are wrong.

b

c breaks rule 4. The Diagonal Line across the Square is wrong.

c

a breaks rules 1 and 4. The Cross/Circle type and Diagonal Lines are wrong.

a

e breaks rules 1 and 3. The Cross/ Circle type and fills are wrong.

e

d follows all the matrix rules.

d

d completes the matrix.

Exercise 27: 4c Which figure completes the matrix?

8)

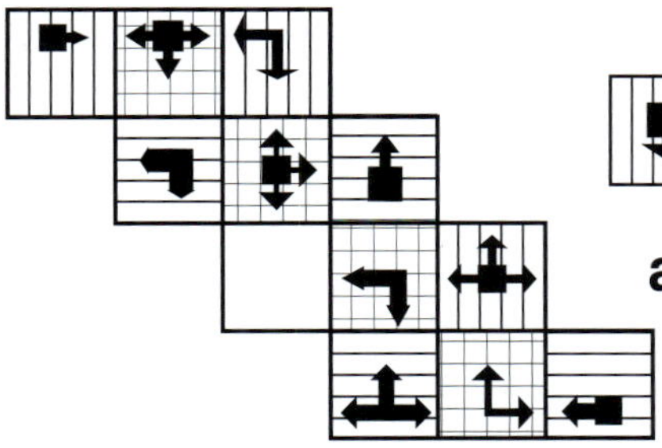

a

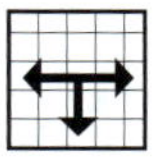

b

c

d

e

Answer a

9)

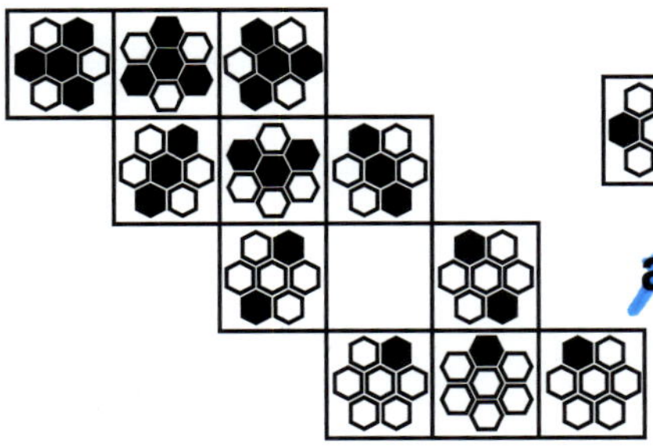

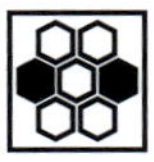

a

b

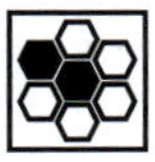

c

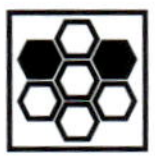

d

e

Answer d

10)

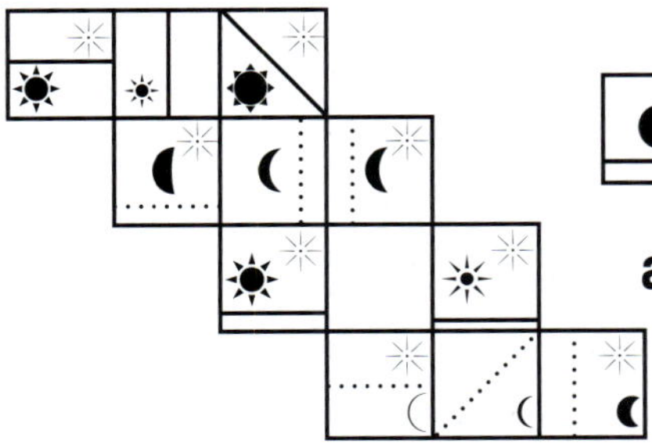

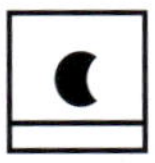

a

b

c

d

e

Answer b

Score

Notes

Answers

Chapter Twenty-three
Recognising Shapes

Exercise 23: 1
1) **b** and **d**
2) **a** and **e**
3) **b** and **c**
4) **b** and **e**
5) **a** and **c**
6) **c** and **e**
7) **a** and **d**
8) **b** and **e**
9) **a** and **e**
10) **a** and **c**

Exercise 23: 2
1) **d**
2) **c**
3) **a**
4) **b**
5) **c**
6) **c**
7) **d**
8) **a**
9) **d**
10) **c**

Exercise 23: 3
1) **b**
2) **a**
3) **a**
4) **c**
5) **c**
6) **b**
7) **a**
8) **a**
9) **b**
10) **d**

Exercise 23: 4
1) **a**
2) **b**
3) **a**
4) **d**
5) **d**
6) **c**
7) **c**
8) **a**
9) **b**
10) **c**

Exercise 23: 5
1) **a**
2) **b**
3) **d**
4) **c**
5) **b**
6) **b**
7) **b**
8) **d**
9) **b**
10) **d**

Exercise 23: 6
1) **d**
2) **c**
3) **a**
4) **d**
5) **b**
6) **c**
7) **b**
8) **a**
9) **b**
10) **d**

Exercise 23: 7
1) **d**
2) **b**
3) **c**
4) **a**
5) **b**
6) **c**
7) **d**
8) **a**
9) **b**
10) **c**

Exercise 23: 8
1) 

2) 

3) 

4) 

5) 

Answers

6) 

7) 

8) 

9) 

10) 

Exercise 23: 9

1) **b**
2) **a**
3) **c**
4) **d**
5) **a**
6) **d**
7) **b**
8) **b**
9) **c**
10) **c**

Exercise 23: 10

1)

1. c	2. g	3. a
4. h	5. f	6. d
7. e	8. i	9. b

2)

1. d	2. g	3. f
4. c	5. e	6. b
7. i	8. h	9. a

3)

1. e	2. a	3. b
4. f	5. d	6. g
7. h	8. i	9. c

4)

1. h	2. f	3. a	4. e
5. c	6. l	7. d	8. k
9. b	10. i	11. g	12. j

5)

1. f	2. p	3. s	4. a
5. e	6. h	7. v	8. x
9. b	10. r	11. n	12. g

6)

1. k	2. o	3. j	4. u
5. i	6. w	7. l	8. t
9. m	10. d	11. c	12. q

7)

1. e	2. l	3. d	4. g
5. j	6. f	7. c	8. a
9. b	10. h	11. i	12. k

8)

1. j	2. h	3. d	4. i
5. e	6. c	7. g	8. a
9. b	10. l	11. f	12. k

9)

1. j	2. a	3. x	4. h
5. e	6. r	7. t	8. u
9. m	10. k	11. f	12. b

10)

1. v	2. o	3. c	4. i
5. p	6. n	7. s	8. q
9. w	10. g	11. l	12. d

Exercise 23: 11

1) **b**
2) **c**
3) **d**
4) **a**
5) **c**
6) **a**
7) **d**
8) **b**
9) **c**
10) **c**

Exercise 23: 12

1) **b**
2) **c**
3) **a**
4) **d**
5) **b**
6) **d**
7) **a**
8) **b**
9) **c**
10) **d**

Exercise 23: 13

1) **a**
2) **c**
3) **b**
4) **d**
5) **b**
6) **b**
7) **b**
8) **d**
9) **a**
10) **b**

Answers

Exercise 23: 14

1) **a**
2) **c**
3) **d**
4) **c**
5) **b**
6) **c**
7) **b**
8) **c**
9) **d**
10) **a**

Chapter Twenty-four
Rotation & Reflection

Exercise 24: 1a

1) **c**
2) **a**
3) **b**
4) **a**
5) **d**

Exercise 24: 1b

6) **b**
7) **d**
8) **c**
9) **c**
10) **b**

Exercise 24: 2

1) 

2) 

3) 

4) 

5) 

6) 

7) 

8) 

9) 

10) 

Exercise 24: 3

1) **b** 90° Clockwise
2) **b** 180° Clockwise
3) **c** 270° Clockwise
4) **d** 180° Anticlockwise
5) **a** 270° Anticlockwise
6) **d** 90° Clockwise
7) **a** 180° Anticlockwise
8) **c** 270° Clockwise
9) **b** 90° Anticlockwise
10) **d** 270° Anticlockwise

Exercise 24: 4

1) **c**
2) **b**
3) **d**
4) **a**
5) **d**
6) **b**
7) **d**
8) **c**
9) **a**
10) **a**

Exercise 24: 5a

1) **e**
2) **b**
3) **c**
4) **d**
5) **a**

Exercise 24: 5b

6) **d**
7) **c**
8) **b**
9) **b**
10) **e**

Answers

Chapter Twenty-five
More Analogies
Exercise 25: 1
1) **b**
2) **c**
3) **d**
4) **a**
5) **b**
6) **c**
7) **a**
8) **b**
9) **c**
10) **d**

Exercise 25: 2
1) **c**
2) **b**
3) **d**
4) **a**
5) **c**
6) **d**
7) **a**
8) **c**
9) **c**
10) **b**

Chapter Twenty-six
More Similarities
Exercise 26: 1
1) **a**
2) **c**
3) **b**
4) **b**
5) **e**
6) **c**
7) **b**
8) **e**
9) **d**
10) **a**

Exercise 26: 2
1) **b**
2) **e**
3) **c**
4) **a**
5) **d**
6) **b**
7) **d**
8) **a**
9) **c**
10) **e**

Chapter Twenty-seven
More Matrices
Exercise 27: 1
1) **d**
2) **a**
3) **c**
4) **c**
5) **b**
6) **e**
7) **b**
8) **d**
9) **a**
10) **e**

Exercise 27: 2
1) **c**
2) **d**
3) **a**
4) **a**
5) **b**
6) **b**
7) **b**
8) **c**
9) **e**
10) **a**

Exercise 27: 3
1) **b**
2) **e**
3) **c**
4) **d**
5) **a**
6) **c**
7) **e**
8) **b**
9) **d**
10) **a**

Exercise 27: 4a
1) **b**
2) **e**
3) **c**

Exercise 27: 4b
4) **d**
5) **e**
6) **c**
7) **c**

Exercise 27: 4c
8) **a**
9) **d**
10) **b**

PROGRESS CHARTS

Shade in your score for each exercise on the graph. Add up for your total score.

23. RECOGNISING SHAPES

Scores

10 9 8 7 6 5 4 3 2 1

1 2 3 4 5 6 7 8 9 10 11 12 13 14

Exercises

Total Score

Percentage

%

24. ROTATION & REFLECTION

Scores

10 9 8 7 6 5 4 3 2 1

1 2 3 4 5

Exercises

Total Score

Percentage

%

25. MORE ANALOGIES

Scores

10 9 8 7 6 5 4 3 2 1

1 2

Exercises

Total Score

Percentage

%

26. MORE SIMILARITIES

Scores

10 9 8 7 6 5 4 3 2 1

1 2

Exercises

Total Score

Percentage

%

27. MORE MATRICES

Scores

10 9 8 7 6 5 4 3 2 1

1 2 3 4

Exercises

Total Score

Percentage

%

Add up the percentages and divide by 5

Overall Percentage %

CERTIFICATE OF

ACHIEVEMENT

This certifies

Nuvvula Neha

has successfully completed

11+ Non-verbal Reasoning
Year 5–7
WORKBOOK **6**

Overall percentage score achieved ______ %

Comment It was so hard and I hate rotitng

Signed Sri [illegible]
(teacher/parent/guardian)

Date The last day of this!